TOCQUEVILLE

AND THE OLD REGIME

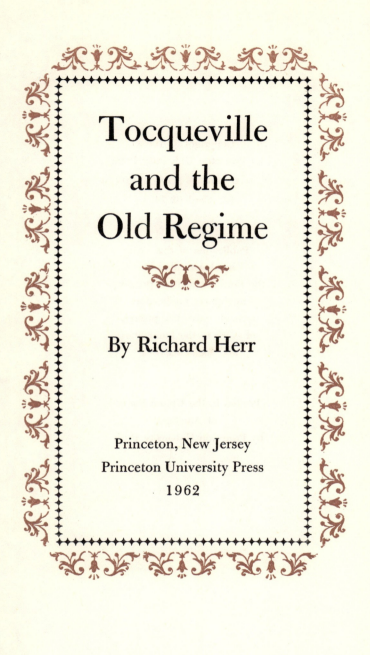

Tocqueville and the Old Regime

By Richard Herr

Princeton, New Jersey
Princeton University Press
1962

TO THE MEMORY OF
MY FATHER

CONTENTS

TOCQUEVILLE

AND THE OLD REGIME

I · THE ARCHIVES OF
TOURAINE

A HAZE that had risen from the Loire River hung tenaciously over the city of Tours one morning in the late spring of 1853 as M. Charles de Grandmaison stepped to the entrance of his prefectural archives to receive a visitor. Before him stood a man of slight, thin stature, with distinguished features. The man's face betokened middle age, and beneath it Grandmaison sensed an inner fatigue. He recognized the visitor at once as a person whose identity had been pointed out to him during his recent training in the manuscript section of the Bibliothèque Nationale. It was M. de Tocqueville, who had come to that institution to engage in research and talk about a book he was writing. Tocqueville's presence there could well have attracted the attention of the staff, for he had been minister of foreign affairs under the Second Republic and had acquired fame fifteen years earlier as the author of a study of democracy in the United States. Grandmaison, like many another young liberal, had read *De la Démocratie en Amérique* and respected its author.

Unaware that he was recognized, Alexis de Tocqueville introduced himself and asked if it were possible to investigate the records of the pre-Revolutionary intendancy of

Touraine. Grandmaison was delighted. Since his recent appointment as archivist of the department of Indre-et-Loire, he had been occupied precisely in putting these records in order and now proudly displayed them to his distinguished client. After thumbing through a couple of bundles, Tocqueville left with the promise to return the following day.

He was back the next morning, bearing a large black leather portfolio such as a former deputy might own, and began to study the correspondence between the one-time intendants and the royal ministers. Each morning thereafter he returned. Word of his visits rapidly penetrated to the adjoining prefecture. In the next days officials of the prefecture began to call at the archives, whose existence had hardly attracted their notice before, explaining that their tasks suddenly required consultation of the departmental records. The real object of their curiosity soon became unhappily aware of their attentions, which kept him from his purpose. Grandmaison smarted for a few days under this unwelcome invasion of his domain and then invited Tocqueville to work in the seclusion of his own private office. Here Tocqueville settled at a battered desk which commanded a quiet view of the prefectural vegetable garden. Henceforth he could study his materials at leisure, untroubled by bureaucratic stares, and Grandmaison could relish a complete monopoly of his guest.

Throughout the summer Tocqueville returned regularly to this spot, while the archivist sought to fulfill his wishes for documents on the old regime. At first Tocqueville hoped to go through the records as far back as Louis XI (the fifteenth century!), but Grandmaison convinced him that such an undertaking was beyond human powers. The older man soon put himself largely in the hands of the young archivist, looking at whatever offered promise that Grandmaison unearthed from the disorder of musty records. From these documents Tocqueville took copious notes, uninterested in turning over to an amanuensis a task that to some might have seemed routine.

Gradually the two men, the kindly author of international renown and the fledgling archivist, became intimate in their collaboration. They would spend the first moments of the morning in conversation, often dwelling on aspects of the project upon which Tocqueville was engaged—a book about the French Revolution, its origins and aftermath. After a scant half hour, Tocqueville would seem to consult an imaginary watch, then break off their chat and turn abruptly to his work. Occasionally as he finished perusing a *liasse* or dossier, he would comment on his findings. Thus the summer passed, and the pile of notes in the black portfolio grew thicker and thicker.

Late in the season Grandmaison had the privilege, possibly unique among the inhabitants of Tours, of an invitation to dinner at the residence of his new friend. Tocqueville and his wife had rented a small country house a few kilometers outside Tours at Saint-Cyr. As he explained to Grandmaison, he had come to Touraine to recover his health, seeking to escape the rigorous climate of Paris. Saint-Cyr was a small town backed up against the rocky hillsides of the northern bank of the Loire, and Tocqueville's residence had the double advantage of being sheltered from the cold winds of the north and west and receiving the full warmth of the sun from the south. Before the southern façade of the house stretched a lawn surrounded by trees, and beyond it a fruit and vegetable garden laid out in formal pattern. A triple row of linden trees at the end hid the nearby river from view, but the spires of Tours were visible in the distance. Tocqueville had christened the place his Hermitage.

On the occasion of his visit, Grandmaison had the opportunity to observe Tocqueville in his domestic setting. In

Mme. de Tocqueville he found a distinguished and charming hostess. If he noticed that she was of English origin, he paid little attention to the fact. Instead he observed how her treatment of her ailing husband seemed to combine the feelings of a wife and a devoted sister. An old friend of the family, M. Jean-Jacques Ampère, was staying with them and joined in the dinner. Tocqueville flattered Grand-maison by remarking that their talks at the archives were helping to settle the plan of his book. The main part of the conversation, however, concerned Ampère's recent journey to the United States, which Tocqueville had not revisited since his trip in the early thirties. The two men discussed the current issue of slavery in that country and expressed fear of an eventual conflict between the north and south over the question.

From his Hermitage Tocqueville went each day on foot to the archives. His walk took him beside the Loire River until he reached the impressive stone bridge of Tours, the second longest in France. It had fifteen arches and had been built under Louis XV and Louis XVI. The four middle arches had been carried away by a spring flood in 1789 and had been replaced at that time by a temporary wooden span. The bridge had not been properly rebuilt until 1810, when the First Empire was at its height. The history of the bridge was easily known to any traveller, and no doubt Tocqueville occasionally lingered as he crossed it and pondered the chronological coincidence between the major events in the life of the bridge and those of the vaster historical subject in which he was engrossed.

As he did, he could look about and enjoy one of the best views Tours had to offer. Straight ahead through the heart of the city lay the imposing Rue Royale, which one contemporary English traveller reported to be "the finest street I have seen in provincial France, . . . very few of those in Paris can compete with it."[1] Off to the left, the twin towers of the cathedral rose above the other buildings, and along the river front in each direction ran a quai, shaded by a line of trees. In summer the Loire was little more than a trickle of water in the middle of a vast dry bed, but verdant islets upstream and down broke the monotony of ugly bars of gravel. To the east progress had recently marred the scenery by erecting a wire suspension bridge. But turning away from it, Tocqueville could admire the steep northern bank, decked with terraced houses, villas, and châteaux. A cluster of these not far downstream was Saint-Cyr, whence he had come. The view was much admired locally. As Tocqueville said, it was "what one calls charming if one has never been out of Touraine."[2] Leaving the bridge, he walked past a newly erected statue of Descartes, rising over the words, "Cogito ergo sum." The philosopher was shown cogitating and, presumably, establishing his own existence. From here Tocqueville followed the broad sidewalks of the Rue Royale, past hotels, shops, and coach offices, until he had to turn off to reach the prefecture.

As long as the weather was good he felt the daily walk helped his health, but when autumn came he had to give up his regular visits to Tours. Nevertheless, he turned up at the archives once or twice a week to consult a document or simply to converse with his young helper. "In America men sometimes travel a hundred leagues to chat with a friend, I can well go about one to pass the time with you," he remarked. Their talk turned occasionally to Germany,

[1] T. A. Trollope, *A Summer in Western France* (London, n.d.), I, 182

[2] A. de Tocqueville to L. de Lavergne, Oct. 31, 1853, *Nouvelle correspondance entièrement inédite d'Alexis de Tocqueville* (*Œuvres complètes d'Alexis de Tocqueville*, ed. Gustave de Beaumont, Vol. VII [Paris, 1866]) (hereafter cited as "*N.C.*"), p. 303

which Tocqueville was planning to visit, and also to French politics, where he revealed an aversion for the recently proclaimed Second Empire. But mostly he spoke about his book and the encouraging progress it was making. The building blocks were falling into place, he could say, and the time to strive for embellishment was at hand.

In April 1854 Tocqueville and his wife left Saint-Cyr. Grandmaison heard little from them until the end of 1855, when Tocqueville sent a letter asking for verification of some data. In 1856 he published *L'Ancien Régime et la Révolution*. Grandmaison wrote him praising the book, and he replied: "Without you and your archives I could not have written the book I have just published. Everything my previous studies had taught me was disconnected. At your side I found the chain of rules I was seeking. Thus I can truly say that the work you praise so highly was made in the little office of which you speak and that it was mainly in our conversations that my mind hit upon the ideas that afterwards became the source of all the rest."

Tocqueville indeed had a fond recollection of his stay at Tours. He journeyed back there shortly after writing this letter expressly to revisit the archives and little office.[3]

[3] Charles de Grandmaison, "Sejour d'Alexis de Tocqueville en Touraine, préparation du livre sur l'ancien régime, juin 1853-avril 1854," *Le Correspondant*, cxiv (N.S., lxxviii) (1879), 926-49. For the description of Tours, [John Murray], *Handbook for Travellers in France* (London, 1848), p. 194; Adolphe Joanne, *De Paris à Nantes et à Saint-Nazaire par la Loire* (Paris, 1867), pp. 170-72; Trollope, pp. 181-82

II · FROM EMPIRE TO
OLD REGIME

L'Ancien Régime et la Révolution was at once recognized by the public as the best study that had been written of pre-Revolutionary France. The century that has passed since it appeared has not seen its prestige shaken. Tocqueville's work provided materials for the pictures of the old regime drawn by such noteworthy and politically distinct historians as Hippolyte Taine and Albert Mathiez. Within the last generation detailed studies of the eighteenth century have discredited some of Tocqueville's conclusions, but the stature of his work instead of shrinking has only grown. Its rank among the masterpieces of historical writing is thoroughly established. Yet its full import has attracted little attention.

If, as Tocqueville wrote Grandmaison, he found during his ten months at Tours "the chain of rules" that holds *Old Regime* together, a knowledge of the evolution of Tocqueville's thoughts in this period would help greatly to understand the final product. Unfortunately, when Grandmaison wrote the account of Tocqueville's visit which permits us to visualize it, he gave few details of their conversations. Probably he had forgotten them, for twenty-five years passed before he recorded the events. Happily Tocqueville also expressed himself in his correspondence, much of which has been preserved and published.

Tocqueville had a frank mind, and the long and detailed letters he wrote convey many of his intimate thoughts and feelings. Like his letter to Grandmaison, they repeatedly reveal an innocent desire to please and flatter his friends. There was no finer and more delicate way to do so than to lay bare his mind to them, and he was always ready to practice flattery on this harmless level. Of course he wrote only what he wanted to have known, but some of his correspondents were friends from youth, and others had shared political misfortune with him. A full and accurate text of his surviving correspondence is only now being edited by the Commision nationale pour l'Édition des Œuvres d'Alexis de Tocqueville under the direction of J.-P. Mayer and André Jardin, but many of his letters were published shortly after his death by his travelling companion in America and lifelong friend Gustave de Beaumont. Beaumont tampered with them, removing passages that seemed uninteresting or too personal; nevertheless what we can see of Tocqueville's letters to his close friends—and it is considerable—can be taken with reasonable assurance at face value as an expression of his own thoughts as he understood them himself.[1] The penetrating critic Charles-Augustin Sainte-Beuve, who had a personal aversion for the author

[1] The volumes of Tocqueville's correspondence edited by Gustave de Beaumont are Alexis de Tocqueville, *Œuvres et correspondance inédites* (2 vols., Paris, 1861) (hereafter cited as "*Corr.*, I," and "*Corr.*, II") and *N.C.* (see above p. 7 n.2). Comparison of some of the original letters in the Yale Tocqueville Collection, Yale University Library, New Haven (hereafter cited as "Y.T.MSS"), with Beaumont's version shows that Beaumont omitted extensive passages, especially those concerning personal affairs, and reworded the remainder to cover up his omissions. Until the work of the Commission nationale pour l'Édition des Œuvres d'Alexis de Tocqueville is completed, students of Tocqueville must rely on the mutilated version offered by Beaumont, for the papers of Tocqueville are not open to the public.

of *Old Regime*, was forced to admit after reading the volumes of his correspondence: "No one has ever scrutinized his own thoughts more conscientiously than Tocqueville, no one has ever exposed them more sincerely. Montaigne, who spent his life drawing his own portrait, did not reveal himself more clearly to us."[2] The introspection and candor of Tocqueville's letters allow us to perceive, in part at least, the inner struggles he went through while he was writing his book.

The story of its writing went back at least three years before his visit to Tours, to the days of the Second Republic. After nine years in the Chamber of Deputies under Louis Philippe, Tocqueville had welcomed the Revolution of 1848 with both hope and foreboding. He feared that the drive of the working classes, in which he saw the main force behind the revolution, might bring socialism and an end to personal liberty. But on the other hand, the proclamation of universal manhood suffrage and the maintenance of parliamentary institutions opened up the vista of a free democracy in France.

Ever since he had published the first half of his *Democracy in America* in 1835, he had felt that the greatest trial facing all western nations in his day was the transition to democracy. Would its coming bring freedom or popular dictatorship? These were the only alternatives he could foresee. In 1835 he had concluded his book:

"I am of the opinion that if we do not succeed in gradually introducing democratic institutions into our country, if we despair of imparting to all the citizens those ideas and sentiments which first prepare them for freedom and afterwards allow them to enjoy it, there will be no independence at all, either for the middle class or for the nobility, for the poor or for the rich, but an equal tyranny over all;

[2] C.-A. Sainte-Beuve, *Nouveaux lundis*, x (Paris, 1874), 326

and I foresee that if the peaceable dominion of the majority is not founded among us in time, we shall sooner or later fall under the unlimited authority of a single man."[3]

At first the Revolution of 1848 seemed to follow the right road. The conservative vote of the peasants in the provinces upset the plans of the Parisian radicals to dominate the Constituent Assembly. Tocqueville was elected a deputy from his home district in Normandy, and because of the prestige accruing from his *Democracy* and his experience in the Chamber, he was made a member of the Committee for the Constitution.

But now developments went awry. In June the workers of Paris, sensing their loss of control of the revolution, again brought forth weapons and raised barricades, this time not against a monarchy but their own republic. When the trouble started Mme. de Tocqueville hurriedly left the city, but she managed first to notify her husband, who was in the assembly, that their porter was threatening to kill him. After the session ended, much later than usual, about midnight, Tocqueville returned home through darkened streets, armed with a brace of pistols to defend his slight body against the threats of his burly doorkeeper. This precaution proved unnecessary, for the two men passed the night alone in the building without incident; but having escaped the one danger he had foreseen, Tocqueville was almost killed the next morning when he pushed into the heat of the bitter street fighting.[4] Four days of relentless slaughter finally

[3] Alexis de Tocqueville, *De la démocratie en Amérique (Œuvres complètes*, ed. J.-P. Mayer, Vol. I, Parts I, II [Paris, 1951]), Part I, p. 330. Here and elsewhere I have quoted the translation of *De la démocratie* from the Vintage Book paperback edition: Alexis de Tocqueville, *Democracy in America*, trans. Henry Reeve, ed. Phillips Bradley (2 vols., New York, 1954) (here from I, 342). I have checked this translation against the original and occasionally made some changes in my excerpts.

[4] Alexis de Tocqueville, *Souvenirs*, ed. Luc Monnier (Paris, 1942), pp. 151-55

silenced the guns behind the workers' barricades. Tocqueville's experiences during these fearsome moments were to be among his keenest memories of the Second Republic.

Outward calm returned to France after the June Days, but it did not reassure him. The assembly would not heed his urgent recommendation to provide in the new constitution for decentralized government, a bicameral legislature, and indirect election of the president. He did not like the election in December 1848 of Louis Napoleon Bonaparte as president of the republic. Yet he was still sanguine enough early in 1849 to write to a close friend that he was happy with universal suffrage and that "there is much of an accidental and passing nature [in the election of Louis Napoleon], and those who believe they see in it signs of a permanent character are people of very short sight."[5]

In May 1849 a lifelong dream to hold high political office materialized when he became foreign minister in the ministry of Odilon Barrot. The international position of the Second Republic promptly became ambiguous because Louis Napoleon used French soldiers to destroy a democratic republic in Rome and occupy the eternal city. Some of the discredit that the French republic suffered among democrats everywhere inevitably rubbed off on Tocqueville. Before he could weave the threads of his policy together to his satisfaction and recover his honor by inducing the pope to adopt liberal reforms, Louis Napoleon dismissed the entire Barrot ministry. It was the end of October 1849.[6]

Tocqueville's dismissal was to prove a turning point in

[5] T. to E. Stoffels, Mar. 9, 1849, *N.C.*, p. 239

[6] For Tocqueville's life during these years the standard work is Edward T. Gargan, *Alexis de Tocqueville; the Critical Years 1848-1851* (Washington, 1955). See pp. 128-30, 175; also Alexis de Tocqueville, *Correspondence and Conversations of Alexis de Tocqueville with Nassau William Senior from 1834 to 1859*, ed. M. C. M. Simpson (2 vols., London, 1872) (hereafter cited as "*Conversations with Senior*"), i, 233-40

his life. His inevitable feeling of frustration was followed during the winter by serious illness. Since his days in America, his respiratory system had been noticeably weak. In the winter of 1848-1849 he had been forced to give up work for a month. Now, a year later, a new attack came with frightening symptoms. He coughed up blood.[7] By the end of April 1850 his condition no longer seemed immediately dangerous, but he wrote: "I nevertheless preserve a very unpleasant memory of this illness. It came I know not why, it can return without my being able to preserve myself against its attacks. Fortunately [he added reassuringly] according to the doctors my lungs have not suffered."[8]

His doctors spoke less confidently to Mme. de Tocqueville. They told her that another winter would have to pass without a relapse before he could be considered out of danger. To watch over her husband's health was no new duty to Mme. de Tocqueville. As young Mary Mottley in the care of her aunt, she had first met Alexis when he was a fledgling *juge auditeur* at Versailles in the reign of Charles X. The proud Tocquevilles saw in her only an unattractive English woman, somewhat Alexis's senior, without the background needed to recommend her union to the scion of their ancient family. But he found companionship of the mind in Mary—to him she became Marie—and in 1835 he

[7] Gustave de Beaumont, "Notice sur Alexis de Tocqueville," in *Corr.*, I, 24 (illness in America); T. to G. Grote, Feb. 27, 1849, *ibid.*, II, 144-46 and T. to E. Stoffels, Mar. 9, 1849, *N.C.*, pp. 238-39 (winter 1848-49); T. to Mrs. Grote, July 23, 1858, *Corr.*, II, 449-50 and J.-J. Ampère, "Alexis de Tocqueville," in his *Mélanges d'histoire littéraire et de littérature* (2 vols., Paris, 1867), II, 303 (winter 1849-50). Tocqueville's letters at this time make clear that the illness was frightening: T. to H. Reeve, Mar. 1850, in Alexis de Tocqueville, *Correspondance anglaise* (*Œuvres complètes*, ed. J.-P. Mayer, Vol. VI, Part I [Paris, 1954]) (hereafter cited as "*C.A.*"), p. 112; T. to E. Stoffels, Apr. 28, 1850, *Corr.*, I, 460-61. See also Beaumont, "Notice," *loc. cit.*, pp. 112-13

[8] T. to E. Stoffels, Apr. 28, 1850, *Corr.*, I, 460-61

ignored his family's disapproval and married her. They soon went to live in an old family château in the village of Tocqueville on the Norman coast near Cherbourg. They never had children, and all Marie's tenderness and devotion had been directed to caring for the needs of her gifted but physically weak husband.[9] The responsibility she now shouldered, if more serious than at any previous time, was familiar enough.

Early in June 1850 the couple went to their home in Tocqueville, but before winter came, bringing the dread trial the doctors envisaged, she took him to Sorrento in southern Italy. Jean-Jacques Ampère joined them there and shared Mme. de Tocqueville's anxious watch. Relaxation, walks, conversation, and absence from the political anxieties of France slowly revived Tocqueville's health. When spring finally came, Ampère and Mme. de Tocqueville sighed joyfully to each other, "Alexis has been saved!"[10]

Their relief was not fully warranted. The later history of Tocqueville's health suggests that he was already suffering from an advanced case of tuberculosis. For the remaining eight years of his life, his activities would be largely determined by his physical condition. Besides his lungs and bronchial tubes, his stomach was to plague him repeatedly.[11]

By the summer of 1851 his strength had revived enough to permit him to return to Paris to resume his tasks as a deputy. He took a leading part in a last attempt to forestall an irreparable breach between the president and the assembly. But now the anxiety he had felt in 1848 for

[9] Antoine Redier, *Comme disait Monsieur de Tocqueville* (Paris, 1925), pp. 121-28; George Wilson Pierson, *Tocqueville and Beaumont in America* (New York, 1938), p. 692n., 741; F. A. A. Mignet, *Nouveaux éloges historiques* (Paris, 1877), pp. 81-82

[10] Ampère, *loc.cit.*, p. 303

[11] T. to Beaumont, Oct. 22, 1855, Y.T.MSS, B 1 c

France's freedom overshadowed his hopes of that year, and his gift for prognostication warned him that the republic would not survive the conflict between the executive and the legislative power.[12] Nevertheless, Louis Napoleon's *coup d'état* of December 2, 1851, which disbanded the assembly by force of arms, added a sense of dreadful finality to what had previously been only a premonition. Tocqueville joined 229 other deputies in a vain protest. All they earned for their pains was two cold days and nights in prison.

The eventuality against which Tocqueville had warned France in 1835 appeared to have materialized. French citizens had not acquired "those ideas and sentiments which first prepare them for freedom and afterwards allow them to enjoy it," and so they had fallen "under the unlimited authority of a single man." In Tocqueville's eyes, the French people themselves were to blame for vitiating their democracy by rejecting freedom, for he judged December 2 not as the victory of an astute planner but as the work of the people. A "coup d'état populaire" he termed it even before it occurred.[13] His definition proved accurate. Except for a few persons in Paris, almost no one stirred in defense of the assembly. A plebiscite on December 21, 1851 approved Louis Napoleon's destruction of parliamentary government by seven and a half million to six hundred thousand votes.

For nearly two decades France was to be governed by a strong executive, who would soon change his title from president to emperor. Although Louis Napoleon maintained a legislature, he modeled it on the docile chambers of the First Empire, and its role was to seem unimportant in the political scene until after 1860. Henceforth the centralized

[12] See T. to Beaumont, Jan. 29, 1851, *Corr.*, ii, 171
[13] T. to Beaumont, Sept. 14, 1851, *ibid.*, pp. 177-78. See also T.'s conversation with N. W. Senior on Dec. 23, 1851 in *Conversations with Senior*, ii, 7

administration created by Napoleon I would have much more apparent authority. It enjoyed extensive police powers and could now proceed to ferret out political opponents of the regime, unhampered by accountability to regular courts or parliamentary opposition. Louis Napoleon could justify his political system by the overwhelming endorsement given by plebiscites to the changes he made in the constitution.[14] The prospect of a "Caesarian democracy" of this kind had long stirred horror in the heart not only of Tocqueville but of nineteenth-century liberals as a whole.

Tocqueville suddenly felt how far his own ideas were removed from those of the majority of his countrymen. "Are we not strangers in France?" he wrote Odilon Barrot. To another friend he likened their situation to that of the Jews in the middle ages, and to a third he confided: "I perceive that there is almost no more point of contact between the way of thinking [of my compatriots] and my own. I have kept strong tastes that they no longer have, I love passionately what they have ceased to love . . . . I find myself an old man in the midst of a new people." He wrote to Gustave de Beaumont: "I would indeed be upset if I were less sad. On this score I have no complaints, for in truth I am sad unto death. I have reached my present age through many different happenings but with only one cause, that of regular liberty. Will this cause be lost without recourse? I feared so already in 1848; I fear so more today. Not that I am convinced that this country is destined never again to see constitutional institutions; but will it see them last, them or any others? We are made of sand. One should not ask whether we shall remain stationary but only what are the winds that will blow us about."[15]

[14] On the aspects of administrative tyranny, see Howard C. Payne, "Theory and Practice of Political Police during the Second Empire in France," *Journal of Modern History*, xxx (1958), 14-23

[15] T. to O. Barrot, July 3, 1852, *N.C.*, p. 287; T. to an unnamed

His dismissal from the ministry and his subsequent illness had made him feel the weight of his years. He was in
his late forties. "My youth has gone, and time marches on,
or rather runs down hill toward ripe old age."[16] The passing
years, his ill health, and the sad state of France became
inextricably intertwined in his troubled mind. His correspondence seldom mentioned his own condition or that of
his country without at the same time alluding to the other.
A simple sentence he wrote in September 1853 epitomized
his melancholy: "I do not believe that I shall ever see my
own complete cure any more than that of France."[17]

Yet Tocqueville's persistent urge for public recognition
did not perish with his happiness. When he began to suspect that he would never be allowed to lead his countrymen politically toward free democracy, his thoughts turned
to the other field in which he had won acclaim. "I have
thought a hundred times that if I am to leave any traces
of myself in this world, it will be far more by what I shall
have written than by what I shall have done."[18] He used
the leisure provided by his convalescence from his illness
of 1850 to write his recollections of the Second Republic,
but he realized that their intimate nature would not allow
publication, at least not during his lifetime. And his spirit
needed the solace of public acclaim while he was still of
this world. At Sorrento in the winter of 1850-1851 he conceived of a work that would match his *Democracy* or even
surpass it, for he felt better qualified after ten years in politics "to treat well a larger subject of political literature."

correspondent, June 16, 1852, quoted in Albert Gigot, "M. de Tocqueville," *Le Correspondant*, LI (1860), 715-16; T. to Comtesse de Circourt, Sept. 2, 1853, *Corr.*, II, 230-31; T. to Beaumont, May 1, 1852,
ibid., p. 185
    [16] T. to L. de Kergorlay, Dec. 15, 1850, *N.C.*, p. 259
    [17] T. to M. de Corcelle, Sept. 17, 1853, *Corr.*, II, 225
    [18] T. to Beaumont, Jan. 10, 1851, *ibid.*, I, 81

"But what subject to take?" he rhetorically asked his boyhood companion Louis de Kergorlay. "More than half the chances of success lie in finding the correct answer, not only because I must find a subject that interests the public but especially because I must find one that inspires me and brings out everything that I can give." Only one such subject could exist, the French Revolution, the revolution which, he said, "goes from 1789 to our own days."[19]

How could he treat such a vast topic? He felt that the best way would be a short volume on the First Empire, "the cause, the character, and the significance of the great events that form the principal links in the chain of that time." What he would seek to portray was not "the acts themselves, however surprising or grandiose they are, but the spirit of the acts."[20] A statement he made to an English friend at this time suggests that in taking up the study of the First Empire he was motivated less by an interest in the French Revolution than by his fear of Louis Napoleon. Speaking of the first Napoleon, he said: "He subdued anarchy, he restored our finances, he did much to which France owes in part her power and her glory. But he deprived her not only of liberty, but of the wish for liberty; he enveloped her in a network of centralization, which stifles individual and corporate resistance, and prepares the way for the despotism of an Assembly or of an Emperor."[21] Whatever light an analysis of the First Empire might shed on the French Revolution, what better means was there in 1851 to an understanding of the genesis of a second empire?

[19] T. to Kergorlay, Dec. 15, 1850, *N.C.*, pp. 258-60
[20] First quotation from T. to Beaumont, Jan. 10, 1851, *Corr.*, I, 82; second from project outlined at Sorrento, Dec. 1850, "Les projets de Tocqueville," in Alexis de Tocqueville, *L'Ancien Régime et la Révolution*, ed. André Jardin (*Œuvres complètes*, ed. J.-P. Mayer, Vol. II, Parts I, II [Paris, 1952]) (hereafter cited as "*A.R.*, I" and "*A.R.* II"), Part II, p. 301
[21] *Conversations with Senior*, I, 113

Tocqueville left Sorrento with little accomplished on this new project, and he did not take it up again before the *coup d'état*. For a few months after the coup he debated staying in politics on the local level, but he renounced the idea because present conditions would not allow him to "make an effective opposition."[22] The end of his political life left him psychologically more than ever in need of another occupation. Early in 1852 he turned to his book on the First Empire as the last resort to end his depression. He stayed in Paris through the spring and undertook research apathetically in the Bibliothèque Nationale. But, he confided to Beaumont, "despite all my efforts at distraction, I feel a constant bitter sorrow that overcomes me."[23]

That summer he returned with his wife to their home on the Norman coast in hopes that the move would revive his spirits. The château stood on one of several properties that belonged to his family. The spot was especially dear to him because it was the ancient seat of the Tocquevilles, who had been seigneurs of the village since remote days and derived their title from it. The most impressive feature of the château was two round granite towers with walls six feet thick that dated from the middle ages. One of these stood at the southeastern corner of the building and was used for living quarters. The other, rising directly behind the central doorway, enclosed a massive winding staircase. Around these two towers the rest of the house had been constructed about the time of Louis XIII in the neoclassic style of that age. At some distance from the body of the château a third granite tower stood roofless. Before the great Revolution it had been used by the Tocquevilles to house thousands of pigeons—one of their seigneurial privileges consisted in

[22] T. to Reeve, Aug. 8, 1852, *C.A.*, p. 135. See also T. to Barrot, July 3, 1852, *N.C.*, pp. 286-88
[23] T. to Beaumont, May 1, 1852, *Corr.*, ii, 185. See T. to V. Lanjuinais, Apr. 18, 1852, *N.C.*, pp. 280-81

having the only pigeon-house in the village. During the Revolution the local peasants had done no harm to the seigneurial property except to kill the pigeons and gut the tower, thus destroying this symbol of aristocratic privilege at the same time that the Revolutionary legislators were abolishing the privileges themselves.[24] The Tocquevilles had not rebuilt the tower, and Alexis had managed to overcome by tact and diplomacy the hatreds and suspicions that the peasants of his day had inherited from the old regime. He now basked in as high a regard among his local inferiors as his medieval ancestors had ever enjoyed.[25] As he retreated from Paris and its frustrations to his château, the atmosphere of his aristocratic background could be expected to do more for his constitution than more balmy air could ever have done.

The château had suffered neglect during Tocqueville's recent absence, and he had to call in workmen. In order to write he was forced to withdraw into a room in the corner tower. His work did not proceed easily. He was upset by the loss of some notes during his trip from Paris, but he confessed to Beaumont that the real cause of his trouble lay deeper. "I do not yet know well whether or not I have a subject, but I am seeking it with desperate energy. Because, without the resource of a great book to write, I really wouldn't know what to do with myself."[26]

He succeeded in composing two chapters dealing with

[24] T. to Reeve, July 24, 1837, *Corr.*, II, 71-72; *Conversations with Senior*, I, 99, 102, II, 221-22
[25] See his description of his election in 1848 in *Souvenirs*, pp. 100-101; and Louis de Loménie, "Publicistes modernes de la France, Alexis de Tocqueville," *Revue des deux mondes*, 2e période, XXI (1859), 419-21
[26] T. to Beaumont, July 16, 1852, *N.C.*, p. 289. For his daily life, T. to Reeve, Aug. 8 and Sept. 3, 1852, *C.A.*, pp. 134-35, 137; and for his loss of notes, Beaumont to T., July 3, 1852, Y.T.MSS, D I b, 5e cahier

the rise of Napoleon;[27] but after this brief productive spurt he bogged down. In September he wrote: "I study, I experiment, I seek to grasp the facts more tightly than I feel others have hitherto done, in order to squeeze from them the universal truths they contain. I have not yet hit upon a plan, and I have written nothing that can be called the beginning of a book."[28] In October he and Mme. de Tocqueville journeyed back to Paris. He was immediately forced to bed with pleurisy.[29] Before he was on his feet again, Louis Napoleon had proclaimed the Second Empire and Tocqueville had given up writing the history of the First.

By January 1853 he was concerned instead with "the beginning of our revolutions, or rather [he added, repeating one of his constant ideas], our revolution, since there is only one, which still goes on and is not yet near its end."[30] He was searching now for a background to the Napoleonic system of administration. Driven on by the added sorrow of the revival of the Bonapartist empire, he plunged into "an ocean of researches," mostly in the records of the généralité of the Île de France.[31] But try as he would, he could not fasten upon a proper subject for a book, and all his efforts could not take his mind off contemporary events. By April "the sadness that the sight of my country causes me and my apprehensions for its future" had again undermined his constitution. This time the hardships of the situ-

---

[27] "Comment la République était prête à recevoir un maître," and "Comment la nation en cessant d'être républicaine était restée révolutionnaire," *A.R.*, II, 269-92. See T. to Kergorlay, July 22, 1852, *Corr.*, I, 384; Beaumont to T., Aug. 16, 1852, Y.T.MSS, D I b, 5e cah.; André Jardin, "Note critique," *A.R.*, II, 13

[28] T. to Comtesse de Circourt, Sept. 18, 1852, *Corr.*, II, 197

[29] T. to Senior, Nov. 13, 1852, *N.C.*, pp. 292-93

[30] T. to Baron de Bunsen, Jan. 2, 1853, *Corr.*, II, 198

[31] T. to Beaumont, Mar. 3, 1853, *ibid.*, pp. 202-3. See also his MS note quoted in Jardin, *loc.cit.*, p. 15

ation, both physical and moral, had also damaged his wife's health.[32]

Ill, discouraged, his nerves on edge, with little to show for a year's work, and still disoriented, Tocqueville decided to try the climate of the Loire valley, which centuries earlier had enticed the Renaissance kings of France away from Paris. The move would also bring him close to his dear Beaumont. Beaumont himself took charge of finding a furnished house that would suit the spiritual and bodily needs of his ailing friend, and after a lengthy exchange of letters the two finally agreed on a secluded country estate in Saint-Cyr that Beaumont described as a perfect place to relax and worship the sun.[33] Late in May the Tocquevilles left Paris for this new Eden. Their arrival was somewhat marred by a continuous pouring rain and the anguishing nocturnal discovery that they were the welcome guests of a colony of half-starved bedbugs;[34] but summer soon drove away the rain, the Tocquevilles succeeded in doing as much to the insects, and Alexis could thereafter speak affectionately of the place as his Hermitage.

Was it hope or desperation or just plain courage that brought him to Grandmaison's archives within days after his arrival at Saint-Cyr? Was a hint of the subject that he despaired of finding already knocking about in the back of his mind? In turning his attention to the old regime, he did not have to explore entirely strange ground. In 1836 he had published in the *London and Westminster Review* a long article on "The Political and Social Condition of France."[35]

[32] Quotation from T. to Bunsen, May 23, 1853, *Corr.*, II, 204-5. See also Beaumont to T., Feb. 5, 1853, Y.T.MSS, D I b, 5e cah.; T. to Reeve, Mar. 26, 1853, *C.A.*, p. 145; *Conversations with Senior*, II, 35-36

[33] Beaumont to T., Apr. 19, 1853, Y.T.MSS, D I b. 6e cah.

[34] Beaumont to T., June 3, 1853, *ibid*.

[35] [Alexis de Tocqueville], "Political and Social Condition of France," *London and Westminster Review*, xxv (1836), 137-69, re-

It had dealt entirely with the old regime, for subsequent articles he had planned on the period after 1789 were never written. Moreover his father, Count Hervé de Tocqueville, had in recent years published a two-volume *Histoire philosophique du règne de Louis XV* and a briefer *Coup d'oeil sur le règne de Louis XVI.*[36] Alexis had always felt a strong attachment to his father. Count Hervé had been the respected prefect of Versailles when Alexis was beginning his career as a local magistrate. Even though they had seen each other infrequently after the Revolution of 1830, his father's study of the old regime must have sharpened Alexis's interest in the period.

If he now had a suspicion that he might end up with a book on the old regime, he refused for some time to admit such a possibility to others and even to himself. Soon after his arrival at Saint-Cyr he wrote that he had found "a precious deposit for what I have undertaken to do," which was, to become thoroughly familiar with the old regime in order to perceive its influence on the Revolution. But "it would be a great mistake to strive to paint the old regime itself." From his growing pile of notes all that would come forth was "a little chapter of thirty pages."[37] Late in October, after five months of research, he still jestingly proposed to a friend in Paris: "If you would be so kind as to ask the minister of public education, who is favorably disposed toward me, to establish a chair for me at the Collège de France in the administrative law of the old regime, I believe I am up to filling it fairly well. But shall I ever make use of all this jumble? I truly fear not."[38]

---

printed in the original French as "État social et politique de la France avant et depuis 1789" in *A.R.*, ɪ, 33-66

[36] The first is Paris, 1847, the second, Paris, n.d. On Alexis's relations with his father see Pierson, pp. 17-18

[37] T. to M. Freslon, June 9, 1853, *Corr.*, ɪɪ, 207-9

[38] T. to L. de Lavergne, Oct. 31, 1853, *N.C.*, p. 305

Nevertheless the jumble continued to knock about in his mind and intrigue him more and more. During the summer he had been led to consider the differences between the previous condition of France and that of its neighbors. He already knew something of England, through his reading, visits to the country in the 1830's, and his English wife. Now he read William Blackstone's classic *Commentaries on the Laws of England* and wondered, not for the first time, why the English nobility had developed into an "aristocracy" while the French had become a "caste." As a possible explanation he considered the fact that England, unlike France, had never experienced administrative centralization.[39] He concluded he would have to look also at the past evolution of Germany if he were to understand what had happened in France. He decided to make a special trip to that country. Since he knew little German and since Beaumont, with whom he was in constant touch, was busy learning the language, he began to study it too, "just as if I were a twelve-year-old."[40]

As late as October, however, his attempts at writing continued to be discouraging. Yet he already felt his trip had been rewarded. Mme. de Tocqueville had completely recovered her health, and his was much better. "I cannot say that I lead a gay existence here," he wrote Barrot. "How can one's spirits not be sad in the presence of the sight we have before our eyes? But at least my existence is very calm." He determined not to return that winter to the "sterile agitation" of Paris. "I keep very busy, but up to now I have been preparing myself to write rather than writing.

[39] T. to Senior, July 2, 1853, *Corr.*, II, 210; T. to W. R. Greg, July 27, 1853, *ibid.*, p. 213

[40] T. to Comtesse de Circourt, Sept. 2, 1853, *ibid.*, p. 232. See Beaumont to T., letters of 1853-54, Y.T.MSS, D I b, 6e cah., *passim*, but esp. Mar. 23, 1854; and T. to Mrs. Grote, Nov. 22, 1853, *Corr.*, II, 242

I hope the winter will be more fruitful and that I shall profit more from it than from the summer."[41]

His hope was fulfilled. In January 1854 he wrote Ampère that he had already sketched out the first chapter of his book. The object of the chapter was "to show what was the true aim of the Revolution." And he had begun a second to show how the French Revolution differed from all the others that followed it and why such a revolution had occurred in France and not elsewhere. "From time to time I am as happy with myself and as enchanted with my work as a fool could be, which I hope I am not. At other moments I am at the bottom of an abyss of despair. This chapter contains the product of the immense work undertaken in the past year; the mountain of notes overwhelms and suffocates me."[42] In the next two months he reached the conclusion that instead of two chapters on the old regime at the beginning of a book on the Revolution, he would have to have a whole volume on the old regime. He envisaged it as the first part of a long study that would go to the end of the First Empire. He hoped to have the volume finished while still at Tours, but he left in May 1854 before it was done, and it was not to be in print for another two years. Nevertheless the fact that it was well under way and that his health was far improved combined to make him realize as he left that he had succeeded in "spending my time more agreeably than at any other epoch in my life."[43]

In any case, he still had the observations to make on Germany that he hoped to incorporate into his work. Little

[41] T. to Barrot, Oct. 26, 1853, N.C., p. 302. See also T. to A. de Gobineau, Oct. 11, 1853, *Correspondance d'Alexis de Tocqueville et d'Arthur de Gobineau*, ed. M. Degros (*Œuvres complètes*, ed. J.-P. Mayer, Vol. IX [Paris, 1959]), pp. 200-201

[42] T. to J.-J. Ampère, Jan. 1854, in André-Marie Ampère and Jean-Jacques Ampère, *Correspondance et souvenirs (de 1805 à 1864)* (2 vols., Paris, 1875), II, 232

[43] T. to Hubert de Tocqueville, Jan. 12, 1854, N.C., p. 307. See T. to Edouard de Tocqueville, Mar. 7, 1854, *Corr.*, II, 251

more than a month after leaving Tours, he and Mme. de Tocqueville were in Bonn, where he consulted with professors of the local university. He plunged into the history of German institutions "with a *furia francese* that astonishes my hosts."[44] Had he been able to continue, one might expect that his stay in Bonn would have produced a companion volume on Germany to the one on France that came out of Tours, but the university closed for the summer, and Mme. de Tocqueville was suddenly afflicted with rheumatism. They attempted a tour of Germany, but before they had gone far her condition forced them to return sadly to France. The visit to Germany turned out to be less profitable for his studies than Tocqueville had hoped.[45] He had again shown, however, that if he was seeking fame from his writing, as indeed he admitted, it was not a cheap fame, but one that would survive among those readers who could appreciate painstaking and thorough scholarship.

Mme. de Tocqueville's poor health and his own forced the two again to shun Paris and the climate of Normandy during the winter of 1854-1855. They chose this time the neighborhood of his father's estate at Compiègne. Here he returned to his book, reorganizing, meditating, writing. In April 1855 he went to Paris, where he searched the archives for information that he had found he needed to complete his account.[46]

The coming of summer permitted the couple to go back at last to Tocqueville. They had been absent three years from the surroundings he loved, and now he found that the pleasant cares of putting his estate in order and installing a heating system that would permit him to spend win-

[44] T. to Lavergne, July 29, 1854, *N.C.*, p. 333

[45] T. to G. C. Lewis, Sept. 19, 1854, *ibid.*, p. 337; T. to Senior, Sept. 19, 1854, *Conversations with Senior*, II, 89; T. to Corcelle, Oct. 2, 1854, *Corr.*, II, 272

[46] For the details see Jardin, *loc.cit.*, pp. 18-19

ters in the château diverted him from his main enterprise.[47]
When in the autumn he fell to the task again, he saw the
end of it approaching. Yet new misgivings assailed him. To
Ampère he confided that he was writing "obstinately, passionately, and sadly"; and to Beaumont, "I tremble in advance when I think how very necessary success is for me."[48]
The anguish at feeling himself a stranger in his own country
again seized him and convinced him that success was impossible. "The book breathes a spirit that has become almost
unknown to my contemporaries. I have remained an old
and outmoded lover of liberty in a time when everyone
desires a master. This lack of sympathy between the public
and myself frightens me because the experience of past
ages has taught me that the only books which produce a
sensation when they appear are those in which the author
follows the current of his time and not those in which he
goes against it." "Will I publish it? I am not yet sure."[49]

The psychological need for a new claim to public renown
still moved him too strongly for him to hesitate long about
trying his chances. He went to Paris in February 1856 to
negotiate with a publisher, and at the same time he made
arrangements for the simultaneous appearance of an English translation. While waiting for publication, he added
copious notes to his text, many of them embodying information he had gathered in Germany. At the last minute,
adopting the suggestions of friends who were reading the
proofs, he made changes in the foreword and conclusion.[50]
The French version finally appeared in June 1856.

[47] T. to Senior, July 25, 1855, *Conversations with Senior*, II, 125-
26; T. to Mme. Swetchine, Oct. 6, 1855, *Corr.*, II, 299-300

[48] T. to Ampère, Nov. 25, 1855, quoted in Jardin, *loc.cit.*, p. 19;
T. to Beaumont, Oct. 3, 1855 (dated 1854 by the editor by mistake),
Corr., II, 270

[49] T. to Stoffels, Jan. 4, 1856, *ibid.*, I, 469-70

[50] See T.'s letters to Reeve, Jan.-June, 1856, *C.A.*, pp. 155-81;
Conversations with Senior, II, 132

The story of these years reconstructed from Tocqueville's correspondence shows more clearly than Grandmaison's recollections why he considered his stay at Tours so rewarding. While there he was able to hit on a topic that he could develop into a book. After two years of disheartening wrestling with the subject of the French Revolution, during which he had tried unsuccessfully to attack it through the First Empire, he at last came to grips with it at Tours through the old regime. Once he had broken his own reluctance to write a long work on the old regime, he was able to progress with it slowly but regularly until he gave it to a publisher two years later.

Why did Tocqueville have to change his subject in order to carry through his work? Was it simply that he had chosen at last to begin the story at the beginning, or were there more profound reasons why the old regime proved more fertile than the First Empire? He wrote in May 1856 to Henry Reeve, his English translator: "This book was made in solitude. It is the fruit of profound reflections which are the product of one mind alone unobserved by others. I have shown what I have written to only three intimate friends, of whom none has seen more than half. You will be the first to have all of it in your hands."[51] He exaggerated slightly, for others now also had the proofs, but it seems true that he did not show his entire manuscript to anyone until he had finished writing. Under the circumstances, his correspondence is unlikely to reveal the reason why the old regime turned out to be the answer to his need for a subject. If a reason can be found, it is only by examining the book itself.

[51] T. to Reeve, May 3, 1856, C.A., pp. 171-72

III · ARISTOCRACY OR DEMOCRACY?

THE first edition of *L'Ancien Régime et la Révolution* was divided into a foreword, two books, an appendix, and a section of notes. For the second edition, which also appeared in 1856, Tocqueville divided his second book in two, and subsequent editions regularly have three books. This study will refer to three books, since this form is best known.

The foreword is a general introduction, largely rewritten while the type was being set. In it Tocqueville indicates the purpose of the volume and states that it forms the first part of a general history of the French Revolution, which he hopes to be able to continue. He indicates his sources—publications of the eighteenth century; the *cahiers* or lists of grievances carried by the deputies to the Estates General of 1789; minutes of the meetings of provincial estates; and archives of provincial administrations. He explains that they are too numerous for all to be cited in footnotes; therefore he has placed the most important references in notes at the back of the book.[1]

---

[1] Beaumont suggested putting all the notes at the end of the book to make its reading easier (Beaumont to T., Mar. 26, 1856, Y.T.MSS, D ɪ b, 8ᵉ cah.). I have used the edition in the complete works of Tocqueville now being edited by the Commission nationale pour l'Édition des Œuvres d'Alexis de Tocqueville under the direction of

Toward the end of the foreword he discloses his worry that the public will not welcome the work. "Some will perhaps accuse me of showing in this book an untimely taste for liberty, for which, I am assured, almost no one cares any longer in France." But this love is old in him, he says, and he cannot abandon it now, since only liberty can produce patriotism in citizens and greatness in nations. He makes sure that his readers will understand his implied condemnation of the Second Empire by referring obliquely to the unaccustomed economic prosperity that France was enjoying under Napoleon III and its recent success in the Crimean War: "Democratic societies which are not free can be rich, refined, ornate, even magnificent, powerful by the weight of their homogeneous mass, . . . but what will never be seen in such societies, I dare to say, are great citizens and especially a great people. I am not afraid to state that in those societies the common level of heart and mind will never stop sinking as long as equality and despotism go hand in hand."[2]

Book I is also introductory and brief. It is clearly the

J.-P. Mayer (see above, p. 19, n.20). It contains an "Introduction" by Georges Lefebvre (i, 9-30), a study by André Jardin of the steps Tocqueville took in writing the work ("Note critique," ii, 7-26), an "Histoire de l'influence de l'Ancien Régime" by J.-P. Mayer (i, 335-55), as well as Tocqueville's article of 1836 on the "État social et politique de la France," the chapters on the coming of the Revolution and the rise of Napoleon which he did not live to publish, and miscellaneous notes he had taken on the subject of the Revolution. This edition of L'Ancien Régime is copied from the third edition, in which Tocqueville had made some corrections in style. An appendix gives the changes from the first edition.

[2] A.R., i, 75 (Old Reg., Foreword, p. xiv). I have translated the passages from L'Ancien Régime that I quote, but for the convenience of readers who have English editions, the references indicate in parentheses the chapter in which the quotation occurs and the corresponding page in the Anchor Book paperback edition: Alexis de Tocqueville, The Old Régime and the French Revolution, trans. Stuart Gilbert (New York, 1955). Gilbert's translation is at times so free as to obscure the full meaning of the original.

outgrowth of part of the successful writing that Tocqueville's letters showed him doing through the winter at Tours.[3] In it he opposes the conservative and clerical enemies of the Revolution, who since its early days had condemned it as an antireligious and anarchic movement. The purpose of the work, he indicates, will be to reveal the true nature and significance of the Revolution, as well as to explain why the Revolution broke out in France instead of some other European country.

Book II is the longest of the three, being almost half of the entire volume. It deals with lengthy developments that lay behind the Revolution, some going back as far as the middle ages. Most of the first half (chapters ii to vii) is devoted to a description of the growth of administrative centralization under the monarchy. The rest of the book (chapters viii to xii) deals especially with the class structure of France. It describes the effects of royal tax policies in molding this structure, and stresses the decadence of the aristocracy.

Book III sets forth the way in which the mood of the French people was prepared for the outburst of 1789. It analyzes the message of those eighteenth-century writers called the philosophes and the school of economists known as physiocrats. One of the most brilliant sections in the entire volume is then devoted to showing how royal improvements kindled a demand among the people for speedier and more drastic correctives. "Experience teaches us that the most dangerous moment for a bad government usually arises when it begins to reform itself."[4]

Finally, an appendix describes the government of Languedoc, which Tocqueville presents as an example of those out-

[3] See above, p. 26
[4] A.R., I, 223 (*Old Reg.*, Bk. III, ch. iv, pp. 176-77)

lying provinces that had not fallen fully under royal bureaucratic rule.

Within this general framework the material appears incoherent and disorganized. If there is a general theme to hold it all together, it is not developed in such a way as to strike the casual or even the attentive reader. Most commentators have understood the primary lesson of the book to be that the administrative centralization of nineteenth-century France was not a creation of the French Revolution and Napoleon, but had its roots deep in the old regime. That the royal intendant was the ancestor of the Bonapartist prefect was the implicit lesson from Tocqueville's analysis of the intendants' powers. As Georges Lefebvre, in his recent introduction to *Old Regime*, says, "The progress of centralization" is its "principal theme." Its "idée mère," he adds, is that monarchic centralization brought on the Revolution, which in turn furthered centralization.[5]

Administrative centralization, however, is the primary subject of only the first half of Book II. Lefebvre points also to a second subordinate theme, that of the decline of the French aristocracy, defeated in its struggle to prevent centralization. Yet the decline of the aristocracy is only one aspect of the second half of Book II. The purpose of much of Book II and all Book III remains to be explained.

Book III, of course, might be understood as primarily an introduction to the volume that was to follow on the Revolution. Indeed, the disjointedness of the entire *Old Regime* might at first sight seem attributable to its being a separate part of a greater work. Gustave de Beaumont (and who knew Tocqueville better?) wrote shortly after Tocqueville's death:

"A painting of the old society was not at all his final object. He took from that society only those pictures which

[5] G. Lefebvre, "Introduction," *loc.cit.*, pp. 26, 28

he needed to illuminate and bring into relief the new state, 1789, the revolution, its consequences, the empire, and especially the emperor. Here was the heart of his studies, here the source of his meditations, of his anxieties, of his alternating sorrow and hope. The true title of the work would have been *La Révolution française,* and it is the one Tocqueville would have adopted if he had not been afraid of taking one that was already hackneyed. The French Revolution—there lay his thoughts, the subject that obsessed him, the shadowy abyss into which he aspired to bring light, the formidable problem whose solution he wished to find."[6]

Tocqueville did not settle on a title until after his publisher had the manuscript. For lack of a better idea, he first suggested *La Révolution.* His editor proposed *La Révolution française.* Tocqueville hesitatingly approved, then abandoned this title as being commonplace. He hit instead on *L'Ancien Régime et la Révolution française.* When he consulted Beaumont, who was reading the proofs, the latter objected that the subject of the book was the Revolution, not the old regime.[7] Beaumont clung to his view to the end: Tocqueville's main interest was in the Revolution, and the picture of the old regime in France was not intended to be complete but selective and introductory to a longer work on the French Revolution. Beaumont's interpretation, which has become standard, would account for the lack of a clearly evident pattern in the volume. It is the contention of this study, however, that Beaumont was mistaken, that Tocqueville had gone beyond his original purpose, indeed that the Revolution had never really been his main interest, and

[6] Beaumont, "Notice," *loc.cit.*, p. 87
[7] Beaumont to T., Mar. 8, 1856, Y.T.MSS, D 1 b, 8e cah. On the choice of title see also T. to Ampère, Feb. 1, 1856, in Ampère, *Correspondance*, ii, 282; T. to Reeve, Feb. 28, 1856, *C.A.*, p. 164; and Jardin, *loc.cit.*, p. 20

that the book has a meaning which has seldom been hinted at by its critics. After all, Tocqueville had not particularly favored *La Révolution française* as a title, and (after dropping the adjective "française") he kept the one he had thought of, despite Beaumont's objections.

Like the ocean, *Old Regime* moves on various levels. The whitecaps and waves on the surface are the most apparent. They consist of the description of the government and society of the old regime, the familiar themes of royal centralization and aristocratic decadence. But Tocqueville clearly wants his readers to acquire more than just a picture of France before 1789. He invites us to descend beneath the subjects on the surface to their bearing on the outbreak of the Revolution. Beneath the waves, he seems to say, there is the slow rise and fall of the tides. There he leaves us, but we remain confused if we conclude that his thoughts do not go deeper even than the role of social and political institutions in causing the Revolution. Under both the whitecaps and the tides runs an ocean current, which can be detected only with care and proper soundings.

When Tocqueville's thoughts were taking shape at Tours, he wrote to a friend: "You are familiar enough with my ideas to know that I accord institutions only a secondary influence over the destiny of men. I would to God that I believed more in the omnipotence of institutions! I would have higher hopes for our future, because chance could on some given day then allow us to fall upon the precious piece of paper that would contain the prescription for all our ills, or upon the man who would know the prescription. But, alas! It is not so, and I am thoroughly convinced that political societies are not what their laws make them but what they are prepared in advance to be by the feelings, the beliefs, the ideas, the habits of heart and mind of the men who compose them, and what native disposition and education made these men to be. If this truth does not come forth from all parts of my book, if the book does not cause the readers to look constantly within themselves, if it does not indicate at every instant, without ever assuming a pedagogical air, what are the feelings, the ideas, the customs which alone can lead to public prosperity and liberty and what are the vices and errors which on the contrary invincibly drive prosperity and liberty away, I shall not have attained the principal and, so to speak, the only aim I have in mind."[8]

A year after the appearance of *Old Regime*, he continued to insist on the primacy of beliefs, ideas, and habits of heart and mind, stressing this time that "the movement of ideas and passions" is the only thing that is "absolutely sure in history." "Everything that is specific is always more or less doubtful."[9] Edward T. Gargan, at the end of his recent and thorough study of Tocqueville's thought and life during the Second Republic, notes aptly that for him "the spiritual problem" is "the decisive source in history."[10] A knowledge of Tocqueville's ideas derived from more intimate writing than *Old Regime* thus makes clear that he himself expected his audience to learn more from it than the course of centralization and the decline and fall of the French nobility and the influence of these factors in causing the Revolution. If we wish to see through to the ocean current, we must somehow learn what he has to say in *Old Regime* about "the movement of ideas and passions."

He provides a key in his foreword. After his apology for his unseasonable taste for liberty, he explains:

[8] T. to Corcelle, Sept. 17, 1853, *Corr.*, II, 227-28
[9] T. to Hubert de Tocqueville, Feb. 23, 1857, *N.C.*, p. 437. See also T. to Comte de Circourt, June 14, 1852, *Corr.*, II, 187, and T. to Barrot, July 18, 1856, *N.C.*, pp. 394-95
[10] Gargan, pp. 248-49

"Over twenty years ago, when speaking of
ciety, I wrote almost literally what follows.

"In the midst of the shadows that hide the
can already discover three very clear truths.
that all men of our own day are being driven by
force that we can hope to direct and slow down but not to
overcome. At times it pushes us gently and at others pre-
cipitates us toward the destruction of aristocracy. The
second truth is that among all the societies of the world,
those which will always have the greatest difficulty in long
escaping absolute government are precisely those societies
where there is no longer and can no longer be an aristocracy. The third, finally, that nowhere can despotism produce more pernicious effects than in these societies."[11]

His *Democracy in America*, to which he is here referring
in his first sentence, had indeed been written with this development in mind, but he had then described it in different
and clearer terms. The introduction to *Democracy* states
that the most startling feature he had observed in America
was its social equality. America represented the extreme
development of a pattern that all Christian nations, including France, were following. "In running over the pages of
our [French] history, we shall scarcely find a single event
in the last seven hundred years that has not promoted
equality."[12] This equality of conditions Tocqueville called
"democracy," and he contrasted it with the preceding state
of aristocracy. Throughout his *Democracy*, and especially
in the second part, he found the two basic types of societies
to be aristocracy, marked by social inequality, and democracy, marked by equality. Aristocratic and democratic societies, he asserted, give birth to different political systems.
In aristocracy, political authority is held by the privileged,

[11] A.R., I, 73-74 (*Old Reg.*, Foreword, pp. xii-xiii)
[12] *De la démocratie*, Part I, p. 3 (*Democracy*, I, 5)

propertied upper class. This class defends its liberty and that of its inferiors against the encroachment of any power that seeks to become absolute. In democracy, on the other hand, all persons will have equal political rights. "Rights must be given to every citizen, or none at all to anyone."[13]

Ever since the ancient Greeks, political philosophers repeatedly conceived the basic forms of government to be monarchy, aristocracy, and democracy. Tocqueville has chosen to discard the first member of the triad. Instead he envisages absolute monarchy as only a bridge between medieval aristocracy and modern democracy. In 1836 he explained this development in his "Political and Social Condition of France":

"The people, at the moment when they begin to acquire power, become aware that the nobility directs all local affairs, and they attack provincial government, not only because it is provincial but especially because it is aristocratic. Once local power is seized from the hands of the aristocracy, the question arises of whom to give it to.

"In France it was not only the central government but the king who was given sole charge of exercizing it. . . .

". . . The nations that turn toward democracy begin then ordinarily by increasing the attributes of royal power."[14]

Tocqueville was not the first to eliminate monarchy from among the essential forms of government. Historical developments of the previous century had led others before him to take this step. Although Montesquieu and eighteenth-century thinkers in general had preserved the classic triad, R. R. Palmer has shown that before the French Revolution some perspicacious minds in Europe became aware that the prime political conflict of their day lay between self-perpetuating privileged groups—aristocracies—and those

[13] *De la démocratie*, Part I, p. 52 (*Democracy*, I, 55)
[14] *A.R.*, I, 55

middle class persons who desired an end to status and authority acquired by birth, and who were said to support "democracy." The critical decade of the Revolution made many more people conscious that the struggle of their day was between aristocracy and democracy. Monarchy as an issue tended to disappear along with the head of the French monarch.[15] After 1814 a new king, who had kept his head, returned to France, and the political struggle reappeared as before 1789 between landowning nobles and urban bourgeoisie. The term "democracy," however, was now associated in the public mind with the Jacobins of the Terror, and seemed inapplicable—before July 1830—to the current situation. Nevertheless, the prominent political theorist Royer-Collard said during these years: "If I consider democracy, as one should, in a purely political sense as opposed to, or contrasted with, aristocracy, I must admit that democracy is in flood tide in France."[16]

After his visit to America, Tocqueville was to develop a strong attachment for Royer-Collard,[17] but before 1830 he does not appear to have looked to him for ideas or to have discovered the antithesis aristocracy-democracy. Yet he was reading the debates in the Chamber, and he began to lose his faith in the Restoration monarchy. Soon after his appointment to the bench at Versailles, he met Gustave de Beaumont, another young magistrate of aristocratic origin who, like himself, was questioning his traditional loyalties.

[15] R. R. Palmer, *The Age of the Democratic Revolution, a Political History of Europe and America, 1760-1800*, Vol. I (Princeton, 1959), pp. 13-20 and *passim*; R. R. Palmer, "Notes on the Meaning of the Word 'Democracy,' 1789-1799," *Political Science Quarterly*, LXVIII (1953), 203-26

[16] Quoted in Charles de Rémusat, "De l'esprit de réaction, Royer-Collard et Tocqueville," *Revue des deux mondes*, 2ᵉ période, XXXV (1861), 797

[17] De Lanzac de Laborie, "L'Amitié de Tocqueville et de Royer-Collard d'après une correspondance inédite," *ibid.*, 7ᵉ série, LVIII (1930), 876-911, esp. p. 878

In 1828 Tocqueville wrote a lengthy letter to Beaumont, in which he analyzed the evolution of English history. Here he already contrasted administrative centralization and decentralization. As he was to do in *Old Regime*, he pointed out that feudalism and absolute monarchy had in their day prevailed through much of Europe. He saw that the trend of history had everywhere been toward equality. One senses the influence of the then prominent liberal historian, François Guizot, whose lectures on European civilization he and Beaumont were listening to in rapt admiration. While Guizot saw contemporary society as the product of inevitable progress toward the end of privilege, he did not refer specifically to a struggle between aristocracy and democracy. In his letter on England Tocqueville did not either.[18]

The antithesis does crop up in Tocqueville's writing shortly after 1830. The July Revolution of that year, which drove Charles X into exile and put an end to the rule of the legitimate Bourbon line in France, marked as permanent a turning point in Alexis's life as it did in that of his country. His father ceased to be prefect, and his brothers resigned their public offices rather than serve the man who stepped up to the empty throne. Alexis, however, realized that the clock would never be turned back and believed that even a usurper on the throne was preferable to the alternative, which he believed was a republic and anarchy. With misgivings he took the oath to Louis Philippe, thereby keeping his office. His position soon became none the less intoler-

[18] "Reflections on English History," in Alexis de Tocqueville, *Journeys to England and Ireland*, trans. George Lawrence and K. P. Mayer (New Haven, 1958), pp. 21-41. For Tocqueville's association with Beaumont see Pierson, pp. 19-23, and for his admiration of Guizot, Edward T. Gargan, "The Formation of Tocqueville's Historical Thought," *Review of Politics*, xxiv (1962), No. 1; and Pierson, p. 23. Guizot's ideas on history are summarized in F.-P.-G. Guizot, *Histoire de la civilisation en Europe depuis la chute de l'Empire romain jusqu'à la Révolution française* (nouvelle ed., Paris, 1846).

able. His family was outraged, and his boyhood friend Kergorlay branded him a traitor. On the other hand, his new
masters were not convinced of his devotion. His only solace
was in the knowledge that Beaumont had joined him in
swearing loyalty to the new regime. Late that year, in order
to escape from their growing discomfort, the two young
outcasts conceived a trip to the United States to study recent advances in prison management. They proposed that
the government approve the trip as an official mission, but
months of haggling passed before they received the coveted
authorization. Finally in April 1831, Beaumont and Tocqueville sailed from Le Havre, their spirits excited by the ad-
ventures that they anticipated, for both knew at heart that
prison reform was only a pretext to cover more serious
reasons for visiting America. Tocqueville especially was
reacting to the events of the previous July, which had filled
his imagination with the dangers and possibilities of the
popular rule that France had barely escaped. He wanted
to see what could not be seen in France: what life was like
under democracy.[19]

As it happened, Americans were at this time more conscious than Frenchmen of the dichotomy between aristocracy and democracy. Back in the Federalist period, partisans
of the French Revolution had been labeled "democrats."
Now the descendants of these "democrats" were electing and
re-electing Andrew Jackson, and their opponents had acquired the epithet "aristocrats." Aristocracy in American
ears, of course, did not mean an hereditary nobility. The
fiery senator Thomas Hart Benton enunciated the Jackson-
ian definition of the two terms: "There are but two parties
. . . founded in the radical question, whether People, or
Property, shall govern? Democracy implies a government
by the people. . . . Aristocracy implies a government of

[19] Pierson, pp. 25-44

41

the rich." From the other camp Jeremiah Mason gave the reply: "I know this aristocracy of wealth is apt to be evil spoken of. But in a country where wealth greatly abounds, I doubt whether any other foundation for a stable free government can be found." To this aristocracy of property owners, Jackson was a new Caesar, a representative of democratic tyranny.[20]

This was the atmosphere in 1831 when Tocqueville and Beaumont landed in New York. Because of the expressions he heard from the Americans he interviewed, or the sight of the July Revolution that had been the cause of his trip to America, or the contrast he drew himself between his aristocratic background and America's egalitarian ideal, or because of some other inspiration we may never know, soon after arriving in the United States, Tocqueville was taking down notes in which he contrasted "democratic" principles against "aristocratic" in these terms.[21] When he returned to France and wrote *Democracy*, he made the struggle between aristocracy and democracy the dominant theme of the book.

We now have the key to the foreword of *Old Regime*. When it says, "All the men of our own day are being driven by an unknown force . . . toward the destruction of the aristocracy," it is echoing *Democracy*. They must, that is, be driven toward the only alternative, democracy. Tocqueville had been clearer in his article of 1836. Here too he discussed the growth of royal centralization and the gradual weakening of the aristocracy, and he unhesitatingly spoke of the goal toward which this evolution was heading as "democracy." Strangely, the word "democracy" appears infrequently in the text of *Old Regime*; the uninitiated

[20] Quotations in Arthur M. Schlesinger, Jr., *The Age of Jackson* (Boston, 1946), pp. 125, 13-14. See also pp. 38, 94, 110.
[21] Pierson, pp. 152, 158, 160

reader can hardly suspect that the subject of democracy still deeply concerns its author. Yet there can be no doubt that it does. The notes of *Old Regime*—largely written, like the foreword, after the book was in press, when he was letting his innermost thoughts come out most clearly—refer pointedly to aristocracy and democracy.[22] And in a letter he wrote in 1858 he again spoke of "the two great principles that eternally divide human societies and which, for the sake of brevity, can be designated by the names of aristocracy and democracy."[23] Although the text of *Old Regime* never says so, its great concern is with the transition of France from aristocracy to democracy.

We are nearing the level of the ocean current. The second chapter denies the clerical contention that the Revolution was basically antireligious. The philosophy of the eighteenth century, which was a cause of the Revolution, had as its main object not the destruction of religion, he maintains, but "the natural equality of men, the consequent abolition of all privilege of caste, class, or profession, and the sovereignty of the people." (In terms of the ocean current, the object of the philosophy was simply "democracy.") Nor, he continues, was anarchy the object of the Revolution, as others had said. Anarchy arose because the Revolution aimed not only at destroying the old government but "the old form of society" (we can read "aristocracy"). He remarks that since the middle ages there had always been agitators "who held up the natural rights of humanity in opposition to the constitution of their country." Hitherto their

---

[22] A.R., I, 266, 269, 287, 297, 310 (*Old Reg.* Notes, pp. 224, 227, 254, 267, 285). Speaking of the French and British colonies in North America, Tocqueville says: "Both colonies end up establishing an entirely democratic society; but in Canada, at least while it belongs to France, equality is associated with absolute government, while there [in the British colonies] it is combined with liberty" (A.R., I, 287 [*Old Reg.*, p. 254]).

[23] T. to Greg, Oct. 1, 1858, *Corr.*, II, 456

attempts had failed. "The same firebrand that set Europe on fire in the eighteenth century was easily extinguished in the fifteenth." The reason was that by the eighteenth century "certain changes that had already come about in conditions, customs, and habits had prepared the human mind to hearken to these arguments."[24] Applying the terms of the deeper current: by the eighteenth century, society, which had still been aristocratic in the fifteenth, was becoming democratic. Therefore a democratic political philosophy was welcomed.

At the beginning of Book I Tocqueville asks: What was the true character of the French Revolution? What were its permanent effects? What did it destroy? What did it create? He concludes this book by answering most of these questions. "One sees clearly that the only effect of the revolution was to abolish the political institutions that had for various centuries reigned unchallenged among most European peoples and which are ordinarily designated by the name of feudal institutions [i.e., aristocracy] in order to substitute a more uniform and simple social and political order which had for a basis equality of conditions [i.e. democracy]."[25]

[24] Quotations from *A.R.*, I, 83, 85, 89 (*Old Reg.*, Bk. I, chs. ii, iii, pp. 6, 8, 13)

[25] *A.R.*, I, 95 (*Old Reg.*, Bk. I, ch. v, pp. 19-20)

IV · DEMOCRACY OR
TYRANNY?

THE REVOLUTION destroyed aristocracy and achieved democracy. This is not yet the full import of the ocean current, but, conscious of this much, we can now go ahead into the body of the volume and perceive the depth of the current, the main theme of *Old Regime*.

One of the chapters in Book I shows that the evolution from aristocracy to democracy in France was not unique. The fall of the Roman Empire had bequeathed to the middle ages a social structure and a form of government based on local freedom that were similar throughout western Europe. Everywhere (except in England) by the eighteenth century the power of the princes had grown and the medieval aristocracy "had contracted a senile debility."[1] After having settled what were the true character and purpose of the Revolution, Book I ends with the questions: "Why did this revolution, everywhere prepared, everywhere threatening, explode in France rather than elsewhere? Why did it have here certain characteristics that are not to be found elsewhere or reappear only partially?" To seek the answers is the avowed purpose of the rest of *Old Regime*.

Like so many other aspects of *Old Regime*, these ques-

[1] A.R., I, 93 (*Old Reg.*, Bk. I, ch. iv, p. 17)

tions are misleading. If we succeed in finding the answers to them only (and even these answers are not obvious), we shall not have perceived the depths of Tocqueville's work. Let us again unearth the key by referring to *Democracy*. Recall Tocqueville's Cassandra-like prophecy that if France did not acquire the democratic institutions and the ideas and sentiments that would permit the peaceable dominion of the majority, a single man would eventually entice the people into his despotic grasp. The lesson he attempted to teach in that work was how America had eliminated aristocracy without succumbing to the centralized tyranny against which the local authority of aristocrats had hitherto been the main bulwark.

The omnipotence of the majority he found to be a danger of democracy in America as it was in France and elsewhere. But America had unique features that kept the majority in check. The first was its geography. The vast extent and wealth of the United States created prosperity, and this in turn inspired respect for private property among the citizens. America's vastness and the absence of bellicose neighbors permitted it to enjoy a decentralized, federal government, which protected the people from despotism much as an aristocracy would have done.[2]

More important were institutional factors, including, of course, this same federal government. Local self-rule permitted the flourishing of town meetings and the jury system.

[2] *De la démocratie*, Part I, pp. 88-97, 174, 290-300 (*Democracy*, I, 91-99, 178-79, 298-309). Tocqueville distinguishes between "governmental centralization," which gathers together the authority to enact general laws, conduct foreign relations, etc., and "administrative centralization," by which purely local affairs are decided in the national capital and directed from there. He states that the United States had achieved a high state of governmental centralization while avoiding administrative centralization (*De la démocratie*, Part I, pp. 86-88 [*Democracy*, I, 89-91]). When the present study uses the word "centralization," it means "administrative centralization," which was the phenomenon that worried Tocqueville.

Town meetings gave life to a spirit of self-government, and participation in juries made Americans "feel that they have duties which they are bound to discharge towards society and that they take part in its government." Moreover, the freedom given to the courts to declare legislation unconstitutional "forms one of the most powerful barriers that have ever been devised against the tyranny of political assemblies."[3]

But above all, Tocqueville found that the strongest guarantee of freedom in America was the spirit of its people. In part, this spirit was a product of the institutions—town meetings, jury trial, and freedom of the press—but its roots reached deeper, into the habits and customs of Americans. It arose from the respect of the people for the law, without which the courts would be powerless.[4] It grew out of the habit of associating to protect one's rights and further one's interests. "Voluntary association of the citizens," he pointed out, can replace "the individual authority of the nobles" and protect the community from tyranny and license.[5] Religious devotion, which he found to be another outstanding aspect of the American spirit, served to preach self-restraint and moderation. In America, finally, popular education taught the people, even on the frontier, the truths of religion and their rights under the constitution. "Patriotism and religion are the only motives in the world that can long urge an entire body of citizens towards the same end." Without such a spirit of cooperation, without "the common sense and virtue of the citizens," democracy cannot provide freedom.[6]

In such a view there is much of the eighteenth-century

[3] *De la démocratie*, Part I, pp. 286, 104 (*Democracy*, I, 295, 107)
[4] *De la démocratie*, Part I, p. 153 (*Democracy*, I, 157)
[5] *De la démocratie*, Part I, p. 7; see pp. 197-98 (*Democracy*, I, 10; see 202)
[6] *De la démocratie*, Part I, pp. 94, 124 (*Democracy*, I, 97, 126-27)

feeling about democracy. Both Montesquieu and Rousseau had maintained that democracy could be free only if the citizens had "virtue," and by virtue these two writers meant love of the republic and the desire to serve it. Virtue was patriotism, a willingness of each citizen, in terms of Rousseau's *Social Contract*, to keep the good of the community in mind when making decisions on public policy. According to Rousseau, the citizen must accept a civil religion, which teaches worship of the Supreme Being and reverence of the national constitution or "social contract." In order to keep this virtue alive, marked social inequality must be avoided. An association of small property owners was the ideal basis for democracy according to both Montesquieu and Rousseau.[7]

During his formative years, Tocqueville had chanced to find the works of the French Enlightenment in his father's library. They had shaken the orthodox religious faith implanted in him by the pious family priest to whom his parents had entrusted his early education, and his pleasure in reading them continued throughout his life.[8] In 1836 he wrote to Kergorlay: "There are three men with whom I commune a little every day; they are Pascal, Montesquieu, and Rousseau." Fifteen years later, as he first projected the book that was to become *Old Regime*, he again wrote Kergorlay that he had in mind a work like Montesquieu's *Considerations on the Causes of the Grandeur and Decadence of the Romans*.[9] Given the attraction that Montesquieu and Rousseau had for him, it is hardly surprising that his conception of democracy bore a strong imprint of their

[7] Montesquieu, *De l'esprit des lois*, Bk. IV, chs. ii, iii; Rousseau, *Du contrat social*, esp. Bk. IV, ch. viii

[8] T. to Mme. Swetchine, Feb. 26, 1857, quoted by Redier, pp. 282-88; Pierson, pp. 16-17

[9] T. to Kergorlay, Nov. 10, 1836, *Corr.*, I, 338, and Dec. 15, 1850, N.C., p. 258

philosophy. In one particular he differed from Rousseau. After his youthful apostasy, Tocqueville never recovered his faith in the dogmas of the Catholic religion, but he remained a sincere deist all his life.[10] Nevertheless, thanks perhaps to the teachings of the family priest, perhaps to the influence of his parents, perhaps to his observation of Protestants and Catholics in America or his fears of the lower classes in France, his view of the religion needed by a good democracy was more closely Christian than Rousseau's had been.

Montesquieu and Rousseau, living before the French Revolution, spoke of democracy in abstract terms and did not consider it viable in most existing states, particularly such a large one as France. Tocqueville, however, was wrestling with the immediate problem of reconciling the democratic equality he saw rushing upon France in his own day with the individual liberty it threatened to crush. The dilemma was not easy. America proved the two were compatible, but would they be so in France? Even in 1835 the outlook was bleak. "The democratic revolution has taken place in the body of [French] society without the concomitant change in the laws, ideas, customs and morals which was necessary to render such a revolution beneficial. Thus we

[10] On the controversial question of Tocqueville's religion, see the introduction by J.-J. Chevallier to *Correspondance . . . Tocqueville . . . Gobineau*, pp. 12-15; and Doris S. Goldstein, "The Religious Beliefs of Alexis de Tocqueville," *French Historical Studies*, I (1958-60), 379-93. They demonstrate satisfactorily, at least to me, that although Tocqueville had increasingly strong religious feelings, his disbelief in the Christian doctrines lasted throughout his adult life. Redier, pp. 282-97, and John Lukacs in his introduction to Alexis de Tocqueville, *"The European Revolution" & Correspondence with Gobineau* (New York [Anchor Paperback], 1959) (hereafter cited as *"Eur. Rev."*), pp. 25-28, and in his "Comment on Tocqueville Article," *French Historical Studies*, II (1961-   ), 123-25, uphold the opposite position: that late in life Tocqueville was again a believing Catholic; but they lack convincing evidence.

Lovedy w-out barriers to despotism

have a democracy without anything to lessen its vices and bring out its natural advantages."[11]

Return now to Book II of *Old Regime*. The first chapter points out that feudal rights existed everywhere in Europe in the eighteenth century. Yet they were most hated in France. Why? Because in France the peasants had gone farthest toward shaking off these rights. They owned their land and had been freed from the authority of the seigneurs or feudal lords. The seigneur had become only "un premier habitant." The deepest explanation is that society and government had ceased to be aristocratic and had assumed democratic forms. The remaining fiscal privileges of the aristocracy had thereby become incongruous and unbearable.

The six chapters that follow deal with the famous theme of administrative centralization under the monarchy. What is Tocqueville showing here? During the process of centralizing, which, he points out, fitted the "new social state" (democracy),[12] the monarchy destroyed the old "intermediate powers"[13] and municipal and village liberties; France had once had town self-government similar to that of the United States. (The monarchy, we conclude, although the author does not say so explicitly, eliminated one of the institutions that guaranteed freedom in American democracy.) By "evoking" judicial cases from the regular courts for judgment by royal officials, the monarchy also destroyed the freedom of the courts, their ability to protect the individual from the abuses of the central government. (Another feature basic to American liberties had perished in France.) The kings had repeatedly nullified and violated their own edicts and their solemnly registered patent letters. "One frequently complains that Frenchmen scorn the

11 *De la démocratie*, Part I, p. 6 (*Democracy*, I, 8)
12 A.R., I, 107 (*Old Reg.*, Bk. II, ch. ii, p. 32)
13 A.R., I, 135 (*Old Reg.*, Bk. II, ch. vi, p. 68)

law. Alas! When could they have learned to respect it?"[14] (But in America respect for the law and the constitution, he had found, helped prevent the tyranny of the majority.) Thus in subverting local government, the French monarchy had eliminated institutions that were still alive in America and bore there the burden of the defense of liberty.

This section closes with a chapter on the creation of a great capital in France, one of the results of centralized government. The growth of Paris attracted industry and industry attracted workers. "As for the true danger to which such an agglomeration could give birth, no one foresaw it. Thus Paris had become the master of France, and the army was already assembling that would become the master of Paris."[15] (The old regime, after creating the political machinery for democratic despotism, had attracted the mob that could seize the machinery.) "No citizen of the United States imagines that the people of New York could decide the fate of the American union. . . . Nevertheless New York contains as many inhabitants today as Paris did when the Revolution broke out."[16]

Book II now turns abruptly to the social aspects of the old regime. The discussion opens with a chapter showing how men had become more similar in France than elsewhere. The aristocracy had declined while the middle class had risen. "Basically, all the men placed above the people resembled each other. They had the same ideas, same habits, same tastes, devoted themselves to the same pleasures, read the same books, spoke the same language. They differed only in rights."[17] (French society had become more egalitarian, more democratic—though mark the qualification "all the men placed above the people"—than other

[14] A.R., i, 134 (*Old Reg.*, Bk. ii, ch. vi, p. 67)
[15] A.R., i, 142 (*Old Reg.*, Bk. ii, ch. vii, p. 76)
[16] A.R., i, 139 (*Old Reg.*, Bk. ii, ch. vii, p. 72)
[17] A.R., i, 146 (*Old Reg.*, Bk. ii, ch. viii, p. 81)

societies; therefore a revolution to establish political democracy was more imminent in France than elsewhere.)

At the same time, Frenchmen had become divided against each other as no other people were. In the middle ages the French classes had cooperated in running local government and protecting each other against the crown. But since then the kings had succeeded in driving wedges between the classes. They had done so by a vicious fiscal system. The tax of *franc-fief*, payable by non-noble owners of what had been noble land, made newly rich bourgeois landowners jealous of aristocrats. Peasants had been turned against each other by the odious system of using an individual in each village to collect taxes from his neighbors. Each year this task was assigned to a new man, who would in his turn incur the wrath of his equals. Within the towns and cities, meanwhile, the sale of municipal offices to raise funds for the royal treasury had created local oligarchies. These officials became fearful of their jealous inferiors. Worst of all was the *taille*, the heaviest tax in France, levied on peasants but not on nobles. Noblemen no longer had the duties of governing, but they kept the privilege of exemption from taxation. Hatred and envy of the noble had poisoned the heart of the peasant. (In Book III Tocqueville will say that the sight of aristocratic privileges "had ignited democratic envy in the hearts [of Frenchmen] and it burns there still.")[18] *Democracy* had stressed the importance of cooperation, association, and mutual support among American citizens in the defense of their freedom. In contrast, Book II of *Old Regime* concludes that in France "the division of the classes was the crime of the former royalty and later became its excuse [because Frenchmen could no longer work together in self-government]. . . . It is not a small

[18] A.R., I, 244 (*Old Reg.*, Bk. III, ch. viii, p. 204 [where "l'envie démocratique" is translated "jealousy of the 'upper class'"])

undertaking to reunite fellow citizens who have lived for centuries as strangers or enemies and to teach them to conduct their affairs in common. . . . Even in our own day their jealousies and hatreds live after them."[19]

When he was working at Tours, Tocqueville wrote a letter saying: "I believe I have drawn from this study many new facts and views that explain not only why this great revolution occurred in France, why it had the character we have observed; but, more, why many later events have occurred, and whence have come down to us a crowd of habits, opinions, and preferences which we think are new and which have their roots in the government of the old regime."[20] It now becomes clear why he maintained he was writing about "the feelings, the beliefs, the ideas, the habits of heart and mind" of Frenchmen. Hatred and fear instead of love and respect, "a narrow individualism in which all public virtue is stifled"[21] instead of cooperation: these were the passions he saw around him in the France of his own day, and they were the legacy of the old monarchy.

How different was the case of England! There, Tocqueville states, Englishmen had preserved self-government at the local level, where all classes worked in harmony to further their mutual needs. Classes had not become so similar in their tastes and habits as they had in France; but to resist the extension of central power, the English aristocracy, far from cutting itself off from its inferiors, as the French aristocracy had done, remained open to new recruits and tolerated intermarriage with commoners. This was precisely its virtue, which, Tocqueville complained, few Englishmen or foreigners sufficiently appreciated. (Was he recalling his family's opposition to his marriage with the commoner,

[19] A.R., I, 166-67 (*Old Reg.*, Bk. II, ch. x, p. 107)
[20] T. to Edouard de Tocqueville, Mar. 7, 1854, *Corr.*, II, 252
[21] A.R., I, 74 (*Old Reg.*, Foreword, p. xiii)

Mary Mottley?) "Everywhere that the feudal system was established on the continent of Europe, it developed a caste, only in England did it turn out an aristocracy."[22] And because England had an aristocracy which worked with the other classes in the tasks of local government, English liberty remained alive. England was incomprehensible to Frenchmen. Tocqueville recalls the case of a nobleman who emigrated during the Revolution and found only food for ridicule in such English foibles as preferring to see a rebellious citizen go unpunished rather than create a royal police force. Even Montesquieu, who so appreciated English liberty, failed, Tocqueville says, to perceive that its true basis was in such foibles.[23]

The light that shone in England was not completely extinguished in France before the Revolution. "Liberty was alive, but it was a strange kind of liberty, of which it is hard now to form an idea."[24] It lived among the nobles, who could still hold their heads erect before royal officials. It flourished among the clergy, who did not hesitate to proclaim that no Frenchman should pay a tax to which he or his representative had not consented. The bourgeoisie had its share of liberty, obtained by the ownership of public office, which kept judges from servility in the face of royal power. Frenchmen did not yet know what it was to bow before an illegitimate authority simply because it had the power to help or to injure them. It was this spark of liberty that "created the proud and daring spirits who would make of the French Revolution an object of admiration and terror

[22] *A.R.*, I, 147 (*Old Reg.*, Bk. II, ch. ix, p. 82)
[23] *A.R.*, I, 136, 147-48 (*Old Reg.*, Bk. II, chs. vi, ix, pp. 70, 82). See also the note on pp. 308-10, which compares the irrationality of the English legal system with the rationality of the French one, yet concludes that the English system is preferable because it protects the individual against the state, whereas this protection is lacking in France (*Old Reg.*, pp. 283-86).
[24] *A.R.*, I, 168 (*Old Reg.*, Bk. II, ch. xi, p. 108)

for future generations. It would indeed be strange if virtues so manly could sprout in a field where liberty was no more." "Would to God that we could have preserved, with their prejudices and their defects, a little of their greatness!"[25]

But even this liberty had become vitiated. "It was an irregular and intermittent kind of liberty, always held within the limits of the classes." Worse, it was not shared by the common people. "The people alone, especially those of the countryside, were almost never in a position to resist oppression by other than violent means."[26] We can understand beneath Tocqueville's description that this kind of liberty was not conducive to mutual help and association. Freedom such as this, alive only in privileged groups, could not properly prepare France for democracy.

There was little in the old regime that could. French society was nearing democratic equality, centralized government had largely destroyed the local authority of the nobles, but the institutions that in America had lived on to assume the aristocratic role of preventing tyranny had been perverted in France, and the spirit of voluntary cooperation that was basic to free democracy had been squeezed out of the French people. We have at last descended to the ocean current. The title of the tenth chapter of Book II is, "How the destruction of political liberty and the barriers erected between classes brought on almost all the ailments from which the old regime perished." These words are at the level of the tides. At the level of the current they would read, "How the destruction of political liberty and barriers erected between classes made France unfit for freedom under democracy."

If this depressing conclusion is the true burden of Book II, what is there left to say in Book III?

[25] A.R., I, 177, 176 (*Old Reg.*, Bk. II, ch. xi, pp. 120, 119)
[26] A.R., I, 176, 175 (*Old Reg.*, Bk. II, ch. xi, pp. 118, 117)

V · LIBERTY OR EQUALITY?

THE UNDERLYING PURPOSE of Book II is not readily apparent; that of Book III is even more difficult to fathom. Again, Tocqueville's loose organization is partly to blame. When in preparing for the second edition he divided the second book of his first edition into two parts, he placed in the first of these (now called Book II) "the ancient and widespread conditions that prepared the great revolution" and in the second part (Book III) "the individual and more recent facts that finished determining its location, its birth, and its character."[1] In this latter category he included the first three chapters of Book III, which deal with the philosophy and irreligion of the eighteenth century. Although they concern more recent developments, their real function is to conclude the basic theme of Book II.

The first of these chapters expands what the volume has said earlier about eighteenth-century thought. The sight of outworn and irrational privileges led writers to a political philosophy based on "the natural equality of conditions."[2] It was inevitable, Tocqueville feels, that political philosophy should eventually follow society in becoming

[1] A.R., I, 193 (*Old Reg.*, Bk. III, ch. i, p. 138). In the first edition this statement occurs at the end of Book II, chapter xii, instead of at the beginning of the next chapter.

[2] A.R., I, 195 (*Old Reg.*, Bk. III, ch. i, p. 140)

democratic. But it was not inevitable that the philosophers of the eighteenth century should conceive "an imaginary society in which everything appeared simple and coordinated, uniform, equitable, and in conformity with reason."[3] Why had the French flown to abstractions, instead of attempting to accommodate old institutions to new needs, as the English had succeeded in doing? Because they were deprived of active daily participation in the Estates General and the institutions of local government. The writers, and in their wake the nobles, the middle class, and the people, lost their attachment to the real society and traditional constitution of France and became enamoured of an abstract system drawn from reason and natural law. Even the members of the royal government were misled. "Only the interplay of free institutions can fully teach statesmen . . . how to judge what goes on in the mind of the masses and to foresee what will come of it."[4] Thus the withering of political freedom bred conditions that would further hamper the re-establishment of freedom.

Tocqueville carries this analysis further in the third chapter, where he deals with the physiocrats, those eighteenth-century economists known to history primarily for propounding the doctrine of *laissez faire*. Their recommendations were indeed new in Tocqueville's eyes—they envisaged all the social and administrative reforms later accomplished by the Revolution—but they were not liberal individualists. On the contrary, they saw in "the State" (no longer "the king," Tocqueville points out) the only proper agency for reform. The local bodies, parlements and estates, enjoyed only the physiocrats' scorn for their impotence:

"That peculiar form of tyranny that is called democratic despotism, which had been unknown in the middle ages,

[3] A.R., I, 199 (*Old Reg.*, Bk. III, ch. i, p. 146)
[4] A.R., I, 198 (*Old Reg.*, Bk. III, ch. i, p. 144)

was already familiar to them [the physiocrats]. No more hierarchy in society, no more distinct classes, no more permanent ranks; only a people made up of almost identical and fully equal individuals. Legitimate sovereignty assigned only to this confused mass, which has carefully been deprived of all faculties that would permit it to direct or even watch over the government. Above the mass, a single representative, delegated to do everything in its name without consulting it. . . . In theory its subordinate agent, in fact, its master."[5]

The result of all this philosophy was the *cahiers* of 1789. When Tocqueville read them attentively, he found "to his horror" that they added up, detail by detail, to a demand by the people of France "for the simultaneous and systematic abolition of all the laws and all the usages that were current in the country." "Unfortunate men! They had forgotten even the maxim that their forefathers had expressed four hundred years earlier in the fresh and vigorous French of that time: 'Seek too much freedom and liberty and ye shall receive too much servitude.'"[6] These chapters form a major segment in the line of thought that runs from Edmund Burke's original anathema on the French Revolutionaries for rejecting tradition in favor of abstract reason, to Hippolyte Taine's verdict that they had been blinded by the principles of an abstract "classic spirit."

Chapter two of Book III seeks the cause for the disparagement of organized religion in the eighteenth century. Tocqueville did not find it, as one might have expected, in the lives of the clergy of the time. In fact he had earlier made the point that the individual clergymen were enlightened and "national" on the eve of 1789. They championed liberty and exhibited "public virtue" as actively as did the

[5] A.R., i, 213 (*Old Reg.*, Bk. iii, ch. iii, p. 163)
[6] A.R., i, 197-98 (*Old Reg.*, Bk. iii, ch. i, p. 144)

leaders of the middle class.[7] Neither did the cause for the attacks of the philosophers lie in the religious teachings of the church. No, it was her worldly position that brought the church under fire, according to Tocqueville. Neglecting her proper vocation, she had become a submissive client of the crown. Out of self-interest she now led the defense of the old order and thus aroused the wrath of the prophets of the new. Again, a disastrous effect. In England political wisdom in the eighteenth century led all parties to support the church. In America "the respect for religion is considered the strongest guaranty for the stability of the state and the safety of individuals." But in France: "The universal discredit into which all religious beliefs had fallen at the end of the last century exercised without a question the greatest influence on our Revolution . . . . Nothing contributed more to giving its features the terrible expression that they bore."[8]

Toward the end of the third chapter, Tocqueville at last leaves the problem posed in Book II—why France had become unfit for free democracy—and begins to reveal the topic that is to be the heart of Book III. The physiocrats preferred reform to liberty. Twenty years after the physiocrats began to call for reform, he says here, the spirit of liberty awoke among Frenchmen.

The occasion is the royal abolition of the parlements in 1771—those courts of law wherein dwelt much of that strange kind of liberty to resist the crown that was present in the old regime. This leveling of the last barrier to royal whim produces a profound stir in the people in favor of self-government. The cause soon finds a champion in none other than the king of France. Louis XVI, coming fresh and youthful to the throne in 1774, is swept along by the

[7] A.R., I, 172-73 (Old Reg., Bk. II, ch. xi, p. 114)
[8] A.R., I, 205, 207 (Old Reg., Bk. III, ch. ii, pp. 153, 155-56)

current. He becomes passionately concerned with the welfare of his subjects and takes an active part in governing. Old laws are not changed, but their enforcement is relaxed so as to remove the sting of their inequality. Edicts of reform appear, and their preambles denounce the injustice of the regime of privileges and class differences. Guilds are momentarily abolished, thereby showing workers how they can be freed from their masters. Peasants are invited to discover for themselves the extent of the tax exemptions of the upper classes. At the same time the upper classes become concerned for the welfare of their inferiors.

Unparalleled prosperity seizes the nation, despite all the remnants of past absurdities in government. Why? Because on the one hand there is a government that remains powerful enough to maintain order while ceasing to be despotic, and on the other there is a nation that is "in its higher classes already the most enlightened and most free on the Continent." "If one were to describe the old regime as it was in the last years of its existence, one would produce a very flattering but unrecognizable portrait."[9]

Louis XVI goes further and attempts to decentralize the administration and set up local self-government that will provide training in the use of liberty. In 1787 royal edicts create provincial assemblies that take over major powers of the royal intendants. Louis restores to the towns and villages the right to collect their taxes.

In sum, Louis attempts by waving his absolute wand to establish the prerequisites of free democracy. (These are the words of the ocean current; they are not to be found in the text.) As Tocqueville states in Book II: "Not one [French king] can be found who made an effort to reconcile the classes and unite them otherwise than by subjugating them all in equal submission. I am mistaken, one

[9] A.R., I, 222, 221 (*Old Reg.*, Bk. III, ch. iv, pp. 174, 173)

alone wished to do so and even devoted himself to the task with all his heart; and that one—who can fathom the judgments of God?—that one was Louis XVI!"[10]

Alas! The noble endeavor failed. In part it failed because its leaders did not proceed intelligently. Louis continued like his ancestors to teach vicious practices by example. He trampled on the rights of private property, and he did not respect existing laws. His reforms themselves showed how traditional (aristocratic, free) institutions could be scornfully set aside. The aristocrats were no wiser. Their sympathy for the people did not lessen their disdain. They offered to contribute money to the roads, they did not offer to give up their immunity from taxation. "They abandoned the useful part of their rights and carefully kept the odious part."[11] In the end, to establish local self-government without equality of taxation served only to excite existing jealousies and hatreds.

This ineptness, however, was not really the decisive factor. Democracy by royal fiat did not reunite the classes because the disunity was already too strongly ingrained. "C'était trop tard," Tocqueville moans.[12] Louis's well-meaning attempts only lit the fuse of the great explosion that was to take his own life.

"It was this desire to introduce political liberty in the midst of ideas and institutions that were incompatible with it but that had become ingrained in our tastes and habits —it was this desire that has, over the last sixty years, produced so many vain attempts to create free government, followed by such disastrous revolutions. Finally, tired by so much effort, disgusted by such a painful and sterile undertaking, many Frenchmen abandoned their second ob-

[10] A.R., I, 166 (*Old Reg.*, Bk. II, ch. x, pp. 106-7)
[11] A.R., I, 229 (*Old Reg.*, Bk. III, ch. v, p. 184)
[12] A.R., I, 242 (*Old Reg.*, Bk. III, ch. vii, p. 201)

jective [political liberty] in order to return to their first [efficient administration and social equality] and found themselves welcoming the realization that to live in equality under a master still had, after all, a certain attraction. Thus it is that we resemble much more today the economists of 1750 than our fathers of 1789."[13]

The theme of Book III is that the move to bring freedom and democracy to France did not begin with the Revolution but with the reign of Louis XVI. That first attempt failed because of pre-existing conditions, and so would the Revolution and every succeeding attempt. The France of Tocqueville's day, subservient before its Napoleonic master, he concludes, was not the product of 1851 or 1848 or even 1799 or 1789. It had been conceived and nurtured for centuries under the old regime.

✦

By the end of the volume Tocqueville has answered the questions posed in Book I. France was the original scene of the European revolution and felt its effects most violently because the old feudal society and government had decayed further than elsewhere in Europe. The revolution had to break forth in fury because ties no longer existed between "the more civilized classes of the nation" and "the more uneducated and rough ones."[14] As soon as the old powers had been destroyed, the common people, who had been concentrated in Paris, seized the authority that the kings had gathered together almost as if to invite its seizure. Without respect for religion, without training in liberty, hating the upper classes, the common people led the Revolution to violence. Taine's picture of the bloodthirsty Jacobin is already implicit in Tocqueville.

[13] A.R., I, 216 (*Old Reg.*, Bk. III, ch. iii, pp. 167-68)
[14] A.R., I, 246 (*Old Reg.*, Bk. III, ch. viii, pp. 206-7)

This explanation is on the level of the tides, as deep as Tocqueville expressly takes his readers. Beneath this conclusion is that of the current: by the reign of Louis XVI the transition from aristocratic to democratic society was more advanced in France than in other European countries, while at the same time the public spirit and the institutions necessary for free political democracy had been destroyed by the kings. Those causes which *Old Regime* maintains brought on the Revolution served actually—in Tocqueville's scheme of history—to render France unfit for the society of the future. This is the implicit conclusion of *Old Regime*. Passages that embody it dot the work and establish its existence as icebergs in temperate latitudes reveal the presence of a current from the north.

At last we can see why Tocqueville's change of subject during his stay at Tours made possible the writing of his book. To the question that plagued him after the failure of the Second Republic—Why had French democracy ended in tyranny rather than liberty?—he had found the answer not in the quarter century of the Revolution and Napoleon, as he had originally thought to do, but in the old regime.

VI · FROM POLITICS TO
HISTORY

BENEATH the problem of the causation of the Revolution
we have discovered that Tocqueville's real concern is with
the challenge that has haunted him since the 1830's: the
advent of democracy. This is not the only way in which
Old Regime echoes ideas and convictions that he had held
two decades or more before he wrote this book. Already in
1836 his article on "The Political and Social Condition of
France" described the loss of influence of the nobles over
the people and the growing popular hatred of them. It com-
pared them unfavorably with the English aristocracy. It
pointed to the increasing similarity between the French upper classes, noble and bourgeois. It stressed the growing
atrophy of free local institutions and the centralization of
administration under the crown, and already it made the
point that the Revolution merely completed this labor of
the kings. The article described the older feudal spirit of
liberty in France and the coming of the new democratic
spirit of liberty after 1770. Tocqueville had reached all
these conclusions years before he undertook the writing of
Old Regime.

Certain fundamental premises of *Old Regime* also go back
to this period. One of these is the belief that aristocracy

offered a defense of freedom against the despotic centralization of the absolute state. Tocqueville could have acquired the belief from many sources. From his reading, for instance. Franklin L. Ford and R. R. Palmer have recently reminded us that Montesquieu, Blackstone, the spokesmen of the parlements in their opposition to Louis XV and Louis XVI, and other contemporary writers, both French and foreign, championed the role of hereditary nobility and other privileged orders in defending freedom. In Montesquieu's words: "Abolish in a monarchy the prerogatives of the seigneurs, the clergy, the nobility, and the cities, and you will soon have a state dominated by the people or by a despot."[1] We have seen how devoted Tocqueville was in his youth to the literature of the eighteenth century. He admired Montesquieu perhaps more than any other author, and he read Blackstone during his year at Tours. He could easily have learned the old *thèse nobiliaire* from them.

More personal sources also could have encouraged his penchant for aristocracy early in his life. The aristocratic background of his family was something of which he was keenly conscious; witness the pride he took in the possession of their seigneurial manor at Tocqueville. On his mother's side he had blood ties with former parlementaires. His maternal grandfather had been a judge of the Parlement of Paris, and his great grandfather was the once famous Lamoignon de Malesherbes, a leader of the parlementary opposition to Louis XV.[2] In his article of 1836, Tocqueville quoted one of Malesherbes's most eloquent remonstrances

---

[1] Montesquieu, *De l'esprit des lois*, Bk. II, ch. iv: "Abolissez dans une monarchie les prérogatives des seigneurs, du clergé, de la noblesse et des villes; vous aurez bientôt un État populaire ou bien un État despotique." Franklin L. Ford, *Robe and Sword, the Regrouping of the French Aristocracy after Louis XIV* (Cambridge, Mass., 1953), pp. 222-45, esp. p. 239; Palmer, *Age of the Democratic Revolution*, I, 56-67

[2] Pierson, p. 14

against the king.[3] His family background (though not his family itself, which had become royalist), or his reading, or other less easily surmised sources had inspired in him his faith in aristocracy as the champion of liberty even before he wrote *Democracy*, for this faith was one of its premises.

Not that he was satisfied simply to echo the eighteenth-century apologists of hereditary privilege. After listening to Guizot's lectures on the inevitable march of history toward universal personal freedom and after witnessing the July Revolution, he believed that the day of aristocracy was over. The problem that drove him into studying America was precisely this: how a democratic state could maintain individual freedoms once the nobility was put on a level with the mass of citizens. Again, as has been seen, he owed his basic answers—virtue and community spirit—as much to his appreciation of the eighteenth century as to his observations in America.

These views of democracy and aristocracy were to underlie *Old Regime*. Does this continuity in his ideas mean that Tocqueville learned nothing about French history in the twenty years that elapsed between the publication of his two great works? In a moment of intimacy, he described his historical method in this way:

"When I have some subject to deal with, I find it almost impossible to read any of the books that have been written on the same matter. Contact with the ideas of others agitates and troubles me so much that my reading of those works becomes painful. I abstain then as much as I can from learning how their authors have interpreted the facts that interest me and what are their judgments and the various ideas suggested to them by these facts. . . . Frequently I thus acquire with immense labor what I could have found

[3] *A.R.*, i, 63-64

easily by another means. Having gathered this harvest so painstakingly, I shut the doors on the world, and, as if in a well sealed room, I carefully pass in review all the notions I have acquired by myself. I compare them, link them together, and then I make it a rule to give expression to the ideas that have come to me spontaneously in this long labor without any concern whatsoever for the conclusions that this person or that may draw from them."[4]

Present canons of historical writing, geared to specialization of studies, do not condone the failure to profit from previous historical work on a subject, but otherwise few today could criticize Tocqueville's method. But when he shuts himself off from the world and comes to linking his facts together, he descends beneath the whitecaps to the tides and current. One can wonder if the themes around which his material then "spontaneously" falls into place had not been pre-established long before he began to compose *Old Regime*. Did he, as Sainte-Beuve observes, "begin to think before he learned anything"?[5]

If the answer were a flat Yes, one would be at a loss to explain why Tocqueville experienced the difficult struggle to find a subject which preceded the writing of *Old Regime*. Let us look once more at these years, which were crucial in the creation of the work. This time we must start the story earlier. In the winter of 1850-1851, when he first expressed his wish to write another major work, he envisaged it as an interpretation of the Revolution approached through a close study of the First Empire. This was not the first time he had shown an interest in Napoleon Bonaparte. It can be traced back at least a decade. In 1841 he was elected to the French Academy. The address he was called upon

---

[4] T. to Duvergier de Hauranne, Sept. 1, 1856, *Corr.*, II, 332-33
[5] C.-A. Sainte-Beuve, *Causeries de lundi*, xv (Paris, 1876), 105n. Sainte-Beuve attributes the remark to an unnamed person.

to give at his formal reception dealt, as was traditional, with the career of the late member whom he had been chosen to replace; but he used the opportunity to express his own views on the eighteenth century, the Revolution, and especially Napoleon. The Revolution, he said, destroyed all the old institutions of France. When Napoleon appeared, he was able "to act on a nation as lacking in laws, customs, and habits as if it had just been born." Napoleon reorganized the administration, the judiciary, the civil and political legislation. He made a vast, simple machine of government wherein he alone was the motor. "Nothing like it had ever appeared among any other people."[6]

At this time Tocqueville was giving little of his creative thought to history. The second part of *Democracy* had appeared in 1840. By then he had already turned from the role of observer and political philosopher to that of active politician. He had been elected to the Chamber of Deputies in 1839 by the constituency in which the town of Tocqueville was located.[7] From that date until Louis Napoleon dismissed the ministry of which he was a member in 1849, he was absorbed by the everyday conflict of politics.

The conflict of politics, however, did not divorce its participants entirely from history. Ever since the beginning of the Restoration, as Stanley Mellon has shown, partisan political arguments had been fortified by conflicting interpretations of the events that had transpired between 1789 and 1815.[8] In these interpretations, the Revolution regularly ap-

[6] Alexis de Tocqueville, "Discours de réception à l'Académie française prononcé le 21 avril 1842," in his *Études économiques, politiques et littéraires* (*Œuvres complètes*, ed. G. de Beaumont, Vol. IX [Paris, 1866]), pp. 1-23, quotations from pp. 17-18

[7] Mary Lawlor, *Alexis de Tocqueville in the Chamber of Deputies, His Views on Foreign and Colonial Policy* (Washington, 1959), pp. 20-34. Sister Mary Lawlor's volume describes much of Tocqueville's life between his writing of *Democracy* and the Revolution of 1848.

[8] Stanley Mellon, *The Political Uses of History, a Study of the Historians of the French Restoration* (Stanford, 1958)

peared as the greatest event in French history, which wiped out the old regime and created France anew. For the Liberals, the French Revolution was the final triumphant struggle in a long series of struggles against aristocrats and kings in favor of liberty and self-government. But even those who hated the Revolution and condemned its ideals agreed that it was the greatest event in French history, which had destroyed the past they loved and now overshadowed and directed the evolution of France.

Beside the legend of the cataclysmic Revolution, another had grown up, that of the great Revolutionary hero, Napoleon Bonaparte. The former emperor himself furthered the Napoleonic legend in his writings during his captive years at Saint Helena. Since his death the legend had been spread and embroidered by Romantic poets and novelists like Bérenger, Victor Hugo, and Stendhal, by Napoleon's nephew, the interested pretender Louis Napoleon Bonaparte, and even by King Louis Philippe, who hoped that Napoleon's military glory would somehow rub off on his own carefully furled banners. The July Monarchy excited Napoleon worship to new heights in 1840 by transferring the ashes of the hero from Saint Helena to an imposing tomb inside the Church of the Invalides at Paris.[9]

The legend considered Napoleon as not only the great military leader who had defended the Revolution and carried its ideals to the oppressed peoples of Europe, but also as the organizer of modern France. He had rescued the country from anarchy and achieved the finest aims of the Revolution—social equality and orderly government. In the 1840's this conception of Napoleon was given its most solid foundation by a well-known historian, a politician of the

[9] On the Napoleonic legend see Philippe Gonnard, *Les Origines de la légende napoléonnienne* (Paris, [1906]); Albert Guérard, *Reflections on the Napoleonic Legend* (New York, 1924); J. Lucas-Dubreton, *Le Culte de Napoléon, 1815-1848* (Paris, 1960)

highest rank, a man whom the public could trust, the Or-
leanist leader Adolphe Thiers.[10] Shortly after Tocqueville
entered the Chamber, Thiers retired temporarily from politics and took up his history of the Revolutionary era where
he had left off in the 1820's. The result was the *Histoire du
Consulat et de l'Empire,* whose writing was to extend for
two decades. The first volume appeared in 1845. It described
the achievements of General Bonaparte in the first
months after the coup of 18 brumaire brought him to power.

No accomplishment of the young soldier who had seized
the helm of France in 1799 elicited greater raptures from
his historian than his founding of the national administration. Before 1789, according to Thiers, the government that
France had inherited from the middle ages had degenerated into chaos. The towns and cities were each going its
own way to financial ruin. The Revolutionaries tried to re-
organize the administration, but their efforts produced sheer
anarchy. "There resulted soon a more frightful confusion
than that to which they had wished to put an end." "It was
in such a situation that the First Consul became, one can
say, the true agent of Providence. His clear and accurate
mind, inspired by his resolute and active character, was to
lead him to the true solution of these difficulties." He established the system of prefects, subprefects, and mayors
to transmit to the country the directives of the government,
and at the side of each of these officials he placed a council
to keep him from arbitrary acts and to protect the rights
of the citizens. "Such is this admirable hierarchy, to which
France owes an administration that is incomparable in its
energy, its precision, its financial honesty, and which is so
excellent that it needed only six months to reestablish order
in France, under the guidance, it is true, of a unique genius,

10 Gonnard, pp. 190-221, esp. p. 212; Guérard, pp. 209-11

the First Consul. . . ."[11] Thiers was drawing in greater detail and for a much wider public the picture of Bonaparte the organizer of France that Tocqueville had sketched to the Academy three years earlier. The similarity of the two men's views shows how strongly the Napoleonic legend was gripping French minds in the 1840's.

A year after the publication of Thiers' first volume, Tocqueville was provided with another of the rare occasions he had in this period to marshal his ideas on the French past. The motive was a request of the Academy of Moral and Political Sciences to give an opinion of a new book on administrative law. In his report Tocqueville again spoke of the administration of France as being of recent creation: "In this field nothing resembles that which preceded it; almost everything is of recent date, both the functions and the functionaries. . . . The French administration of our own day is not like that of the old regime. . . ." But his reading of the book on which he was reporting convinced him that Napoleon had received too much credit for the change:

"Almost all our administrative organization is the work of the Constituent Assembly [of 1789-1791]. It posed the principles on which our system rests; its hand fashioned, determined, and gave force to all the agents of our administration. . . .

"All Napoleon did was to preserve or re-establish the system that the Constituent Assembly had founded. He improved it and completed certain parts of it, but most especially he changed its spirit. Wherever the Assembly had placed an executive council Napoleon put a single, subordinate, and accountable agent; wherever it provided for public authority to be conferred by election, he gave the choice

[11] A. Thiers, *Histoire du Consulat et de l'Empire*, Vol. I, (Paris, 1845), pp. 151-53

to the prince. . . . Thus Napoleon succeeded in appropriating to the needs of absolute power that vast machine that had been conceived and fashioned by liberty."

Tocqueville considered the resulting administrative institutions so important that he advised anyone who wished to understand "the ideas, the habits, the acts, the customs, in a word the entire destiny of our nation" to look for their origin in the influence exercised by these institutions. He ended his report by asserting that the challenge of his day was to reconcile the despotic centralization of France with "the morality of representative government."[12]

It was with evident surprise that Tocqueville had learned that the contemporary administration of France was not entirely the work of the emperor. He had come to doubt some of Thiers' dythyrambic eulogy. Yet the change in Tocqueville's outlook was not overly significant. He still unconsciously hearkened to the Napoleonic and Revolutionary legends that were fashioning the thoughts of the men who would make the Revolution of 1848 and bring Louis Napoleon to power—legends that said France had been remade after 1789. He had forgotten that a decade earlier he had judged the ideas and customs of a people to be more influential on their destiny than were their political institutions. His ideas on the history of his country had lost their distinctive character and had largely assumed the commonplace views of the press and forum.[13]

[12] Alexis de Tocqueville, "Rapport fait à l'Académie des Sciences morales et politiques (1846), sur le livre de M. Macarel, intitulé: Cours de droit administratif," in his *Études économiques, politiques et littéraires*, pp. 60-75, quotations from pp. 60, 63, 74

[13] Tocqueville's speeches in the Chamber printed in *Le Moniteur*, Dec. 1, 1840, Jan. 29, 1843, May 31, 1845, and June 10, 1846 and rediscovered by Sister Mary Lawlor refer only occasionally to France's past. When they do, they reflect the concept of 1789 as the great break in French history (esp. Dec. 1, 1840 and May 31, 1845). His letters during these years are equally reticent on the subject of French history.

Because he was steeped in the thoughts of those around him, his first reaction as he saw the Second Republic give way before despotism was to write a book on Napoleon I. His words at the time—"[Napoleon] deprived [France] not only of liberty, but of the wish for liberty; he enveloped her in a network of centralisation, which stifles individual and corporate resistance, and prepares the way for the despotism of an Assembly or of an Emperor,"—echoed the view of the anti-Bonapartists of the time.[14]

Compare with these words the opening phrases of *Old Regime's* discussion of centralization: "In former days, when we had political assemblies in France, I once heard an orator who spoke of our administrative centralization, saying: 'This grand conquest of the Revolution, which Europe envies us.' Far be it from me to deny that this centralization is a grand conquest. I admit that Europe envies us it, but I maintain that it is not a conquest of the Revolution. On the contrary, it is a product of the old regime."[15] Clearly a change came over Tocqueville while he wrote *Old Regime*. He laid aside his Thiers (for who else could be the orator to whom he refers?), he laid aside the other historians of the Revolution, and after the process of solitary meditation he describes himself, he gave expression to the ideas that came to him spontaneously. When he did so, his conclusions turned out to echo his thoughts of the 1830's. But before he could write *Old Regime*, he had to cleanse his mind of the tarnish of more than a decade in politics.

This purification was the essence of his struggle to find the subject for his book. Unaware himself of what was happening, he did not leave written statements showing the process he went through. The reversal of his view on the origins of centralization only reveals the beginning and end

[14] See above, p. 19

[15] A.R., I, 107 (*Old Reg.*, Bk. II, ch. ii, p. 32)

of the process, not the evolution of his thinking in these years. Yet he did furnish indirect evidence of the waning influence of immediate political considerations upon his mind in the changing attitudes he expressed toward class hatreds. We have seen that this was a concern central to his political philosophy.

The starting point for this evolution was the fear of the Parisian working classes that he shared with vast groups in France after the events of February and June 1848. During the winter of 1850-1851 spent in Sorrento to recover his health, he composed his recollections of the Second Republic. Here he pictured the common people of Paris with their socialistic visions as the main danger to French liberty. His recollections are filled with instances of his aversion for them, such as his account of the porter who threatened his life.

This fear clouded the last year of his political career. Six months after writing his recollections he returned to Paris and labored to avoid a final break between Louis Napoleon and the assembly. As the speaker for a parliamentary commission appointed to propose a remedy for the conflict of powers, he put forward an unsuccessful motion calling for the election of a new constituent assembly.[16] But he drew back from the only course that deep within himself he felt might succeed, a dramatic appeal to the people to neutralize the appeal made to them by Louis Napoleon. He refused this course because, as he wrote at the time, "I believe that the Bonapartist current, if it is turned aside, will only be so by a revolutionary current, which will be still more dangerous."[17] Thus at this point, when he was also conceiv-

[16] Gargan, *Alexis de Tocqueville*, pp. 203-17. Tocqueville's report to the assembly is in his *Études économiques, politiques et littéraires*, pp. 574-606.

[17] T. to Senior, July 27, 1851, *N.C.*, p. 271. See Gargan, *Alexis de Tocqueville*, pp. 217-18.

ing the project of a great historical work, horror of the lower classes was so acute in him that it paralyzed his resistance to a new Napoleonic despotism.

In the summer of 1852, after the *coup d'état* of December 2 had driven him out of political life and he had retired to his Norman château to write his book, his first successful effort produced two chapters on the advent of Napoleon Bonaparte in 1799. The theme running through them is that fear among the French people brought Bonaparte to power —fear of liberty, whose effects they had already felt too acutely during the Revolution, combined with fear of a return of the old regime. Caught between fear of the Jacobins and fear of the royalists, France turned to a master who would save her—and enslave her. Was Tocqueville regretting his own fear during the previous year, or was the calm of historical study causing him to forget it?

Two years later he had given up the subject of the First Empire and had outlined the body of *Old Regime*. He was in Germany. In a letter to a friend he gave his impressions of the country. The Germans, he found, despite "all the stupidities they have just undertaken to acquire political liberty" (a reference to their unsuccessful revolution in 1848), nevertheless still loved and respected liberty. "It is the absence of this faith [in liberty] that is the most frightening symptom of our [French] illness and that I do not see appear among these people." What a difference between the countries! The terror of socialism present in France was lacking in Germany. "I have heard no one say that a policeman should be stationed at everyone's door to keep his neighbor from pillaging him and cutting his throat."[18]

When *Old Regime* appeared, fear and class hatred had become in the mind of the author the evil legacy of the former monarchy. They were the opposite of the community

[18] T. to Mme. de Corcelle, July 22, 1854, *Corr.*, II, 258-62

spirit he found essential to good democracy. Yet only five years earlier, faced with the threat of Louis Napoleon, he had given concrete evidence of the same lack of class solidarity that *Old Regime* condemned. In these five years, as he withdrew from active participation in affairs to calm meditation on them, he gradually shed his fears and came to criticize the feelings he himself had shared. His letters and other writings of this period give no indication that he recognized his own inconsistency or the change his spirit had undergone.

One recalls that when he first proposed undertaking a new book, he wrote his friend Kergorlay that the experience of public life had improved his ability to accomplish a project of this kind.[19] Edward Gargan has also concluded from his close study of Tocqueville in the Second Republic that the maturing influence of his political career prepared him to write a great work of history.[20] Doubtless Tocqueville was more mature and had more experience of the world than when he wrote *Democracy*, but the immediate effect of his parliamentary life had not been to improve his historical perspective. Filled with conflicts of the day and worries over the near future, his years in politics had clouded rather than clarified his understanding of the past. Like those around him he had been gripped by the Revolutionary and Napoleonic legends.

Only when his political life was cut short, did the ideas of his youth—his own ideas—gradually recover their hold over his mind. Between 1851 and 1854 he not only found the subject for a book, he found himself again, or at least his own historical philosophy.

[19] See above, pp. 18-19
[20] Gargan, *Alexis de Tocqueville*, pp. 245-50

VII · THE SKILL OF THE KINGS
OF FRANCE

FOR A DOZEN YEARS Tocqueville allowed the ideas on French
history that he had held in the 1830's to lie buried and forgotten in the recesses of his mind, and only after much anguish did he unearth them in order to incorporate them in
Old Regime. If this simple analysis sufficed fully to explain
the origin of *Old Regime,* then Sainte-Beuve's charge that
Tocqueville began to think before he learned would still
appear to be valid. Was it indeed possible for Tocqueville
as he wrote *Old Regime* to splice the lines of this thought
directly onto those he had held before he entered parlia-
ment? Does *Old Regime* consist simply of his earlier ideas
writ large? Or had his experiences in politics left an indel-
ible imprint on his mind that passed willy-nilly into his
book?

Old Regime demonstrates a much more detailed knowledge of French history than Tocqueville had before his
long months of research in the archives of Paris and Tours;
that much is obvious. Whereas his article of 1836 is pre-
occupied almost entirely with the breach between the aristocracy and other Frenchmen, by 1856 the author knows
enough to paint all French classes divided within themselves and against each other. The amazingly detailed de-

scriptions of society and government—the whitecaps and waves of *Old Regime*—are largely new. This additional information, however, belongs to the classification of "learning" rather than "thinking." Tocqueville has learned much about France, but such progress is only to be expected.

But probing deeper into the meaning of *Old Regime*, we do find ways in which his thoughts have evolved since his earlier work. There are changes in the lower levels of the book that demonstrate that he has not stopped "thinking." The evolution can be seen in the two themes that are basic to *Old Regime*: centralization and class hatred.

In *Democracy* Tocqueville expressed envy of those nations, like the United States, which enjoyed the blessings of a federal government, but he did not conceive centralization to be inevitably a curse. "A democratic nation may be imagined organized differently from the American people . . . . Might not a democratic society be imagined in which the forces of the nation would be more centralized than they are in the United States, . . . and yet every citizen, invested with certain rights, would participate, within his sphere, in the conduct of the government?" He was convinced that geography prevented certain nations from enjoying decentralization. "A people which, in the presence of the great military monarchies of Europe, should divide its sovereignty into fractional parts would, in my opinion, by that very act abdicate its power, and perhaps its existence and its name."[1]

Clearly he was thinking of France. Centralization had saved it from extinction. At the time he was echoing his father, a royalist by heart and by profession a prefect under the Restoration. When Alexis was in America he had asked his father to describe for him the administration of France.

[1] *De la démocratie*, Part I, pp. 324, 174 (*Democracy*, I, 335-36, 179)

Count Hervé's reply had stressed the need in past ages for a strong monarchy: "This high power is necessary to maintain unity and to prevent each administrative faction from abusing its independence. . . . In a monarchy, surrounded by powerful and jealous states, a center of unity is necessary."[2]

When Alexis wrote *Old Regime*, he had forgotten the threat of hostile neighbors from which only the growing power of the monarchy had been able to save France. Listen to his account in *Old Regime* of the imposition of the *taille* in 1439. He calls it the beginning of the differentiation between England and France: "I dare to assert that on the day when the nation, worn out by the lengthy disorders that accompanied the captivity of King Jean and the madness of Charles VI, allowed the kings to establish a general tax without its approval, when the nobility had the cowardice to let the third estate be taxed provided it was itself exempt, on that day the seed was sown of almost all the vices and almost all the abuses that undermined the old regime during the rest of its life and ended by causing its violent death."[3]

"Lengthy disorders" might be a euphemism for the Hundred Years War and the Burgundian-Armagnac civil war. If it is, Tocqueville had not always been ready to pass over this period so cavalierly. In the sketch of English history that he sent to Beaumont in 1828, he called this age "the most heroic, the most brilliant, and the most unhappy time in our history." "Every event is engraved on my memory, and thence derives that often unreflecting instinct of hate which rouses me against the English." At the time he was working closely with his father and shared some of his sympathy for royalism. His sketch of English history blamed

[2] Quoted in Pierson, p. 408
[3] A.R., I, 160 (*Old Reg.*, Bk. II, ch. x, pp. 98-99)

the irresponsibility of the French feudal levies for France's defeats in the Hundred Years War. "It was only when bitter sufferings had taught the nobility to obey, when the people had been toughened by all manner of affliction, and above all when the money provided by the States General had enabled Charles V to buy the courage of plenty of brave and disciplined adventurers, that the odds became even and the English quit France leaving nothing but their bones behind."[4]

So in 1828. In *Old Regime* he fails to state that the *taille*, like the grants made to Charles V, was voted by the Estates General and—unlike the grants made to Charles V—was voted explicitly to support a standing army that would protect France from a repetition of "the most unhappy time in our history." Instead, *Old Regime* pictures the kings deliberately choosing a levy that would not arouse the opposition of the nobility so that in the future they might tax at will. "All new taxes become *tailles*. Each year the inequality of taxation separates the classes further and isolates men more deeply than they were isolated before."[5] In his article of 1836, Tocqueville had blamed the aristocrats for not keeping the affection of the people. It was they who insisted on their fiscal privileges.[6] In *Old Regime* they become dupes of the kings, who conjured up inequality of taxation and resulting class hatreds the more easily to rule their subjects.

The evolution of the role assigned to the monarchy lies at the center of the change that has occurred in Tocqueville's interpretation of history since 1836. From indispensable defenders of French unity, the kings have turned into inspirers of class hatreds. Tocqueville is now prepared to

[4] "Reflections on English History," *loc.cit.*, pp. 33-35
[5] A.R., I, 161 (*Old Reg.*, Bk. II, ch. x, p. 100)
[6] A.R., I, 38-41

attribute to them a large proportion of the responsibility for the final outcome in France.

Old Regime does not pretend that the kings caused single-handedly the evolution of the French people. To understand their true role, one must look at Tocqueville's theory of historical causation. The foreword to *Old Regime* says that "an unknown force" is bringing about the destruction of aristocracy. Tocqueville had been more explicit in his study of the United States: "Some power superior to that of man" is hurrying men toward democracy.[7] "The various occurrences of national existence have everywhere turned to the advantage of democracy; all men have aided it by their exertions . . . some unknowingly and some despite themselves, all have been blind instruments in the hands of God."[8] Writing a short time after the publication of *Old Regime* about the petty men in the court of France who precipitated the Revolution, he stated: "I admire the power of God, who is satisfied to use such short levers in order to put in motion the entire mass of human societies."[9]

In the 1830's and the 1850's Tocqueville saw God behind the great evolution of the Christian world toward democracy. But once having started society in motion toward its ultimate goal, Tocqueville's God, like the Supreme Being of the Enlightenment, seems content to sit back and observe the human drama. It is in the province of men to decide the nature of the regime toward which they are headed. Tocqueville wrote *Democracy* to help men reach the right goal. "Why [God] is drawing us toward democracy, I don't know, but embarked on a vessel that I did not build, I am

[7] *De la démocratie*, Part I, p. 256 (*Democracy*, I, 263)

[8] *De la démocratie*, Part I, p. 4 (*Democracy*, I, 6)

[9] *A.R.*, II, 116. John Lukacs has published a translation of the chapters written after *Old Regime* in *Eur. Rev.* (see above p. 49, n.10). The corresponding passage is on p. 79. I have made my own translations from these chapters.

at least trying to use it to gain the nearest port," he explained to a friend.[10] In the 1850's he was much less sanguine over the ability of men to steer their ships to the best port. "Individuals," he expounded in a conversation in 1854, referring to men invested with considerable political or military authority, "have on their side considerable power to work mischief, though not often to work good."[11]

It nevertheless remained within the capacity of human free will, in Tocqueville's philosophy, to decide the fate of societies. In the black mood in which he wrote *Old Regime* the kings turned out to be the individuals who condemned French democracy to tyranny. "Almost all the vices, almost all the errors, almost all the fatal prejudices that I have painted [in *Old Regime*] owe in fact their birth or their continued existence or their development to the skill that most of our kings had to arouse men against each other, the more absolutely to rule them."[12]

The outcome could have been different, and there lay the real tragedy that Tocqueville saw. In the spring of 1855, when the body of *Old Regime* had been written, he went to Paris to study materials on Languedoc. The result he placed in an appendix "On the Pays d'États and in Particular on Languedoc." The pays d'états were those provinces which had preserved their local estates and therefore had not been completely absorbed by royal centralization. Of these Languedoc in the south was one of the most independent. Royal power had made its inroads here as everywhere. The king convoked and adjourned the estates and controlled their membership. He could veto their legislation. He had the right to issue decrees. He had an intendant

[10] Quoted in English in Pierson, p. 749, date and addressee unknown. I have translated "la Démocratie," which Pierson leaves in French.
[11] Quoted in *Conversations with Senior*, ii, 61
[12] *A.R.*, i, 190 (*Old Reg.*, Bk. ii, ch. xii, p. 136)

with powers similar to those elsewhere, including authority over the police. Nevertheless, the preservation of local institutions—estates and autonomous city and town administrations—meant that members of the upper classes devoted themselves to deliberation and administration in a free government. The province undertook its own public works and collected its own taxes. In Languedoc there was financial well-being. There was respect for private property. Taxes were fair and were collected equitably. The men of Languedoc cooperated in preserving their liberty, for the *sine qua non* of free government—class solidarity, the spirit of community—was present. "Thanks to the unique nature of the ancient constitution of Languedoc, the spirit of the new times could quietly enter into it and modify it everywhere without destroying anything. It could have been the same everywhere [in France] . . . if the princes had ever wanted other than to become and remain the masters."[13]

Tocqueville's article of 1836 had none of the pessimism of these last sentences. When he wrote it, he felt that the spirit of liberty, once alive in a people, could not be killed by the actions of their rulers. He believed that "the democratic notion of liberty" as he called it—liberty seen as a natural right given to all individuals instead of a privilege associated with certain classes—was the inevitable consequence of the equalizing of the social strata. In France in the eighteenth century, he maintained, this notion had already penetrated the minds of the enlightened classes, and it was felt as an instinct by the people. Absolutism was destined to vanish in the face of this idea: "From the moment that this [democratic] notion of liberty has deeply penetrated the spirit of a people and solidly established itself there, absolute and arbitrary power is henceforth but a material fact and ephemeral accident."[14]

[13] A.R., I, 261 (*Old Reg.*, Appendix, p. 221)
[14] A.R., I, 62

In a buoyant frame of mind, he foresaw freedom in the future of French democracy. Even in the 1830's he had not always been so optimistic, for *Democracy* had warned his countrymen against the danger of one-man tyranny if they did not mend their ways. Nevertheless the future was still undecided, and he hoped to play a leading role himself in assuring freedom for France. In the last years of the Second Republic he began to despair of the future, but until Louis Napoleon's coup he never ceased to believe that the road to liberty was open to the French people if they would only choose to follow it. He was himself passionately engaged in the struggle to reach port before the ship foundered.

We have seen the tremendous blow that the Bonapartist triumph inflicted on Tocqueville's spirit. The loss of hope that he suffered caused him to shift the blame for France's fate. When he wrote *Old Regime*, he could no longer cast on his own generation the responsibility for what had become a national catastrophe. He discovered instead that France had been deprived of the possibility of freedom before his own time, before that of his parents, before 1789. In a sense, Frenchmen of the nineteenth century no longer had free will, politically speaking. Once they had had it, and certain of them had made wrongful use of it to condemn future generations to servitude. Those who had done so were the kings of France.

✦

One can wonder what Tocqueville had left to say in the volume that he planned on the Revolution itself. While *Old Regime* was at the printers', he gave proofs of it to various friends. Several, including Beaumont, objected that the public should know what the rest of his work was to deal with. As a result, a month before *Old Regime* appeared, he rewrote and expanded both his foreword and his conclusion and thereby provided the passages in which his own feelings come out most explicitly.[15] Fulfilling his friends' suggestion, he tells his readers in the final version of the foreword that he subsequently will describe "the epoch of '89, when love of equality and love of liberty shared [French] hearts, when [the French people] wished to found not only democratic institutions but free institutions." Then he will show how "these same Frenchmen came to abandon their first objective and, forgetting liberty, wished simply to become equal servants of the master of the world."[16] Stopping here, he will describe the new society that issued from the Revolution. The main objective will be, however, to explain how 1789—democratic equality with liberty—degenerated into 1800—democratic equality under tyranny.

But the last part of Book III of *Old Regime*—one section that is almost completely new since the 1830's—has already explained the reason. Love of liberty appeared in France well before 1789, with the destruction of the parlements in 1771. Under Louis XVI a peaceable democratic revolution was attempted from the top down, and it was ruined by "democratic envy." The Revolution could do no more than repeat the experience. One of the sections that was added just before publication says that the passion for freedom reached its zenith in 1789, when it was joined by the older hatred of inequality. In that year "Frenchmen were proud enough of their cause and of themselves to believe that they could be equal under liberty. In the midst of democratic

[15] Beaumont to T., May 15 and June 6, 1856, Y.T.MSS, D ɪ b, 8ᵉ cah.; Loménie, *loc.cit.*, p. 425. According to Loménie's account, an unnamed friend of Tocqueville convinced him that the original version did not call attention strongly enough to the love of liberty present in 1789 and embodied in the Constitution of 1791. Very likely Loménie himself was the friend. Mme. de Beaumont visited Paris early in June 1856 and heard Tocqueville read aloud the new version of the foreword.

[16] A.R., ɪ, 72 (*Old Reg.*, Foreword, pp. x-xi)

institutions they therefore erected everywhere free institutions."[17] At this moment they were "torn from individual
egoism and urged on to heroism and devotion." "I have
studied much history, and I can state with assurance that
never have I met with a revolution in whose inception there
was present such sincere patriotism in such a large number
of men."[18] But when religion was forgotten, when anarchy
and popular dictatorship took over, the old habits, passions,
and ideas reappeared.

"The administration of the old regime had beforehand
taken away from Frenchmen the possibility and desire of
helping each other. When the Revolution came, one would
have looked in vain in most of France for ten men who had
the habit of acting together regularly and watching out
for their own defense. . . .

"The first efforts of the Revolution destroyed that great
institution of the monarchy. It was restored in 1800. . . .

"Centralization was snatched from its own ruins and given
new life. . . . The enterprise seemed of mighty daring because men were conscious only of what they were watching
and forgot what they had seen before. When the dominator
fell, the most substantial part of his work remained standing. His government died but his administration continued
alive, and every time since then that we have tried to destroy absolute power, we have succeeded only in placing
the head of Liberty on the body of a slave."[19]

Sainte-Beuve recalls how he once shocked Tocqueville
by speaking lightly of the principles of 1789. He afterwards
avoided Tocqueville because, he says, he did not care to
argue with believers and those principles were Tocque-

[17] A.R., I, 247 (*Old Reg.*, Bk. III, ch. viii, p. 208). On the writing
of this passage see Loménie, *loc.cit.*, pp. 425-26.
[18] A.R., I, 208 (*Old Reg.*, Bk. III, ch. ii, p. 156)
[19] A.R., I, 246, 129, 248 (*Old Reg.*, Bk. III, ch. viii, p. 206; Bk. II,
ch. v, p. 60; Bk. III, ch. viii, p. 209).

ville's articles of faith.[20] Liberty, Equality, Fraternity—for Liberty and Equality to live in harmony, *Old Regime* tells us, though not in so many words, Fraternity must also be healthy. The hatreds bred by the old regime caused the stillbirth of Fraternity. Liberty, left unaided, was devoured by Equality.

This dismal conclusion was in keeping with Tocqueville's humor as he finished the book. In a letter of January 1855 he said that the coup of 1851 "destroyed the liberties of France in a way that seems permanent." "Everywhere," he wrote two months later, "we are leaving the liberty of the middle ages not to enter upon modern liberty but to return to ancient despotism."[21] His terrible discouragement as he labored to complete the volume and his hesitations in publishing it become more comprehensible. To his satisfaction he had answered the gnawing question, Why was France not free? And the answer was more terrible than he had foreseen: France could never long be free. This fatalism is the main ingredient of *Old Regime* that distinguishes it from his earlier works. It is not simply something new that Tocqueville has learned about French history. Despite Sainte-Beuve, it marks a basic change in his "thinking."

✦

"I remember today as if I were still there [he reminisced about this time] a certain evening when a family party had brought together a large number of our near relatives in the château where my father was living. The servants had been dismissed. The whole family was gathered around the fireside. My mother, who had a sweet and ringing voice,

[20] Sainte-Beuve, *Nouveaux lundis*, x, 327

[21] T. to Freslon, Jan. 21, 1855, *N.C.*, pp. 359-60; T. to Baron Hubert de Tocqueville, Mar. 25, 1855 (dated 1854 by the editor by mistake), *ibid.*, p. 322

began to sing a famous air of our civil troubles which re-
counted the sorrows of King Louis XVI and his death. When
she stopped, everyone was crying, not over the many individual hardships that they had suffered, not even over the
many relatives whom we had lost in the civil wars and on
the scaffold, but over the fate of that man, dead over fifteen
years, whom the majority of those crying had never seen.
But that man had been the King."[22]

The recollection of that scene could well be poignant.
The events of the Revolution had made royalists of Alexis's
family. His forebear Lamoignon de Malesherbes, champion
of the parlements in 1771, became the defender of Louis
XVI before the bar of the Convention. During the reign of
terror that followed, Alexis's father and mother were forced
to watch helplessly as her grandfather Malesherbes and her
mother, father, sister, and brother-in-law were led off to
the guillotine from the cell where they had all been impris-
oned; and Alexis's father went on later to serve the Bourbon
monarchs of the Restoration.[23] From early in life, Alexis's
independent spirit was a disappointment to his relatives. In
1830 his family condemned his decision to recognize the
usurper. Now he had convicted the former kings of the
greatest crime possible against their people: the rape of
their freedom. Could he really have anything left to say?

[22] T. to Lady Theresa Lewis, May 6, 1857, *Corr.*, ii, 383-84
[23] Pierson, pp. 14-18

VIII · FROM OLD REGIME TO REVOLUTION

PUBLICATION of *Old Regime* brought Tocqueville little immediate joy. Just as he finished correcting the last proofs, bad news called him to Compiègne, where he had wintered a year and a half before. There he joined his brothers in witnessing the death of their father. He was devoted to his father despite their political differences. In his grief he tried to hold up the publication of *Old Regime*, sensing perhaps that old Count Hervé would not have approved of all it said, but his editor refused his request and the book came out in June 1856.[1] He returned to Tocqueville and awaited the reaction of the public with foreboding mingled with expectation. The friends who had read his book in proof had written enthusiastically about it, but they were obviously favorably disposed.[2] He still felt that the spirit of the public could not welcome it.

Nevertheless the public did welcome it. Beaumont was in Paris early in July and visited the Institute of France, where he saw Tocqueville's fellow members of the French Acad-

---

[1] T. to Reeve, June 14, 1856, *C.A.*, p. 183; T. to Baron Hubert de Tocqueville, July 2, 1856, *N.C.*, p. 388. Beaumont received a copy of *Old Regime* by June 25 (Beaumont to T., June 25, 1856, Y.T.MSS, D 1 b, 8ᵉ cah.)

[2] E.g., Beaumont to T., Mar. 26 and Apr. 23. 1856. Y.T.MSS, D 1 b, 8ᵉ cah.

emy and the Academy of Moral and Political Sciences. "Most of our colleagues surrounded me to speak of your book," he told the anxious author in a letter, "and there was a chorus of praise and admiration that warmed one's heart to hear. . . . All had evidently been gripped by a lively interest, for the questions you discuss resolve problems that we had wondered about a thousand times. . . . Many people tell me that it is the first real book to appear since 1848."[3] Other friends soon deluged Tocqueville with private letters voicing their praise.[4] Then reviews in the periodical press in both France and England acclaimed it. Finally, the most convincing news came from his publisher, who announced the heartening tale of its sales. The first edition, as big as the first three of *Democracy*, was sold out in two months, and that during the doldrums of the summer season.[5]

Relief and joy seized the author. Perhaps he had misjudged the temper of France. The success of his book made him rejoice for his country. "Because," he gloated, "in order for a book as full as mine of the feeling of liberty to find among us so eager a market that feeling must not be as dead as many believe and as some hope."[6] New ideas should be put forth, he added, because eventually, when they seep down to the people—the new political class, which does not read books but which, history shows, is eventually moved by the most abstract ideas—these ideas

[3] Beaumont to T., n.d. but evidently early July 1856, *ibid.*, 7e cah. (out of chronological order in this collection of Beaumont's letters to Tocqueville)

[4] Barrot to T., n.d. (replied to by T. on July 18, 1856, *N.C.*, 394-96) and Edouard Laboulaye to T., July 3, 1856, both quoted in Roland Pierre Marcel, *Essai politique sur Alexis de Tocqueville* (Paris, 1910), pp. 115-17. See also T.'s replies to Charles Montalembert, July 10, 1856; to M. Bouchitte, Aug. 9, 1856; to G. C. Lewis, Aug. 13, 1856, *N.C.*, pp. 388-407; to Kergorlay, July 29, 1856, *Corr.*, I, 388-91; to Corcelle, June 29, 1856; to Charles de Rémusat, July 22, 1856; to Victor Lanjuinais, July 18, 1856, *Corr.*, II, 310-20

[5] T. to Mrs. Austin, Aug. 29, 1856, *C.A.*, pp. 191-92
[6] *Ibid.*

will become "passions and facts." The French Revolution
had not yet reached its end; the outcome might still be
changed. Tocqueville began to speculate that the transfor-
mation might occur even in his own day.[7]

He had said before publishing that *Old Regime* breathed
a spirit of liberty that had vanished from France. Now he
described the book as tending "to revive free and energetic
feelings in discouraged souls and tired and wavering
minds."[8] Of course, it did nothing of the kind. It could
neither exude liberty nor revive a desire for freedom, for
its true burden was that France could never enjoy permanent freedom. He was aware of its dismal conclusion; that
much is clear from the numerous passages in the book in
which the conclusion is expressed obliquely but unmistak-
ably. His strange inconsistency in nevertheless maintaining
that the book preached liberty appears as a new curtain en-
veloping it against the light of understanding. This very
inconsistency, however, provides illumination to clarify the
most obscure puzzle of all: the author's unwillingness to
state his message explicitly.

The ambiguity of his position is revealed most clearly
in an exchange of letters between him and Authur de Gobineau, that *enfant terrible* of the mid-nineteenth century.
The two had known each other for thirteen years. In 1843
Gobineau, then a young man, had briefly assisted Tocqueville in drawing up a report for the Academy of Moral and
Political Sciences. Their ideas soon proved incompatible,
and their collaboration ended. Nevertheless, Gobineau deluged Tocqueville for the rest of his life with lengthy letters all about himself as a diplomat, as a traveller, and as
a founder of the modern belief in the natural supremacy of
the Aryan race. When Tocqueville was foreign minister of

[7] T. to Barrot, July 18, 1856, *N.C.*, pp. 394-95
[8] T. to Lewis, Aug. 13, 1856, *ibid.*, p. 403

91

the Second Republic, he replied to these unlooked-for attentions by furthering Gobineau's diplomatic career. In 1852
the latter published his racial views in *L'Essai sur l'inégalité
des races humaines*, which propounded the doctrine that
the development of human history was predetermined by
the inequality of races.

Long before, in *Democracy*, Tocqueville had denounced
those historians who believe in blind causation (he labelled
them "democratic").[9] When he read Gobineau's *Essai* at
Tours in the fall of 1853, he at once wrote its author rejecting what he called its fatalism and materialistic predestination. To preach fatalism, he argued, was to discourage
people from attempting to improve themselves and to incite
them to all the vices of pride, violence, tyranny, and abjec-
tion that are engendered by permanent inequality. (One is
reminded of the Catholic criticism of the Calvinist doctrine
of predestination.) Revealingly he added: "Perhaps you are
right, but you have seized on the thesis that has always
seemed to me the most dangerous possible to uphold in our
day."[10]

In January 1856 Tocqueville again wrote Gobineau criti-
cizing his ideas. "We no longer have faith in anything, especially ourselves. A work which tries to prove that in this
world man obeys his *constitution* and can scarcely affect
his destiny by his own free will is like opium given to a
sick man whose heart is already slowing down."[11] Almost
immediately after mailing this letter, Tocqueville packed
up his own manuscript, with its strong dose of opium, and
went off to Paris to seek a publisher.

Gobineau received *Old Regime* late that year at his post

[9] *De la démocratie*, Part II, pp. 89-92 (*Democracy*, II, 90-93)
[10] T. to Gobineau, Nov. 17 and Dec. 20, 1853, *Correspondance* . . .
Tocqueville . . . Gobineau, pp. 201-6 (quotation from second letter,
p. 205)
[11] T. to Gobineau, Jan. 8, 1856, *ibid.*, p. 245

deep in Persia. From his reading of it he drew virtually the same lesson as its author: "A people that under a republic, parliamentary government, or empire will forever cling piously to an exaggerated love of state intervention in all matters, a love of state police, of passive obedience to the tax collector, surveyor, and civil engineer, a people that no longer understands municipal administration and for whom absolute, uncontrolled centralization is the last word in good government, that people not only will never have free institutions, but they will never even understand what free institutions are. Actually, they will always have the same government whatever change of name it may adopt. And, since it will always be basically the same, it is better that the government in practice be as simple as possible."[12]

Except for the final expression of approval of the Second Empire, Gobineau's words might have come from *Old Regime*. He gave them as his own, however. He had been antagonized by Tocqueville's admiration for the men of '89, and as a result he had failed to notice how profoundly *Old Regime* agreed with his own conclusion.

Tocqueville, too, failed to recognize his own message in Gobineau's pessimistic verdict. Coming from someone else, especially from so suspect a thinker as the author of the *Essai sur l'inégalité des races humaines*, the view sounded foreign and revolting. He replied furiously: "I, who do not acknowledge either the right or the taste to entertain such opinions about my people and my country, I believe we must not despair of them. In my eyes, human societies, like individuals, take on value only through the exercise of freedom. I have always conceded that freedom is harder to establish and maintain in democratic societies like ours than in certain earlier aristocratic societies. But I would never be bold enough to think that to do so is impossible. I pray

[12] Gobineau to T., Nov. 29, 1856, *ibid.*, p. 274

to God that he never inspire in me the idea that we must despair of success."[13]

The violence of Tocqueville's reaction is awesome, but it helps us to understand why he never clearly stated the theme of *Old Regime*. *Old Regime* demonstrated, if it demonstrated anything, that the internecine hatreds bequeathed to France by the former monarchy precluded the enjoyment of liberty. The book did not suggest that Frenchmen would ever be able to outgrow these hatreds. That is the conclusion reached by Tocqueville's reason, but his emotions rejected the lessons of his reason. By temperament he did not belong, as Gobineau did, to the age of materialist and positivist thought which opened about 1850. He had been brought up in the Catholic faith, with its fundamental assumption of the freedom of man's will, and, as if by reflex, he abhorred an historical explanation that smacked of predestination or inevitability. Moreover, he had undertaken to write his book dreaming of the new fame it would win him. He craved fame as he might an opiate, for the release it would bring from the strain of prolonged ill health and melancholy, but the fame he envisaged was a revival of his reputation as a champion of French liberty. The book he had written denied the value of the role in which he wished to be remembered. As Gobineau told him, it explained and justified the coming of the Second Empire. No more than his background did his purpose in writing the book allow him to make its lesson clear.

He never seems to have become aware of the ambiguity of his position. He realized when he was writing *Old Regime* that he was at times deeply pessimistic and much less frequently almost sanguine, but he had his manuscript before him in both mental states and yet there is no inconsistency in it. The inconsistency is between the book and the

[13] T. to Gobineau, Jan. 24, 1857, *ibid.*, p. 280

pose he assumed apart from the book, and of this inconsistency his correspondence reveals no consciousness. One
is reminded how his fear of the working classes disappeared
after 1851 without his being aware of the change. There was
in him, as in most persons, a considerable capacity for self-
deception. He wrote a book demonstrating the incompat-
ibility of French society and free democracy, and he hoped
it would inspire a love of liberty among Frenchmen and sat-
isfy his craving for fame. Unconsciously he connived with
his hope and his craving to obscure the lesson taught by his
reason. Out of these inner conflicts came the three levels
of meaning we have found in the book.

✦

With his inconsistencies successfully hidden from himself,
he could imbibe the praise that poured in on him and return
to writing with a glowing spirit. Yet he did not sit down
at his desk, at least not immediately. He dreamed of his
next volumes, but the prospect of writing them seemed
harder than for *Old Regime*. He was not yet sure what line
to take, and he gave himself the excuse that it was difficult
to say something new about the French Revolution.[14]

The cares of a landowner were more congenial to his
pleasant intoxication. Throughout the fall and winter of
1856-1857 he spent the days outside, in the fields and mead-
ows, watching workmen whom he had engaged to transform
his run-down holdings into an estate that he could display
with pride.[15] Fences had to be built for cows and horses,
and the problem of pasturing his sheep concerned him. He
wrote to England to inquire about a type of movable fence

[14] T. to Duvergier de Hauranne, Sept. 1, 1856, *Corr.*, II, 331-35
[15] T. to Baron Hubert de Tocqueville, Feb. 23, 1857, *N.C.*, pp.
435-36

that could be shifted about as the sheep exhausted the grass.[16]

Meanwhile Mme. de Tocqueville devoted herself to ministering to her husband's fragile, nervous constitution. In the evening the two would retire to a quiet sitting room before the warmth of a vast ancient fireplace. He had collected here a small library of his best-loved books—they included very few of the nineteenth century—and the couple would enjoy their mutual companionship quietly reading or writing letters until bedtime. Occasionally a guest or two would form part of their circle.[17]

At one point Tocqueville's urge for general housecleaning led him into the family archives. He found records there up to four hundred years old. Fussing through them as he tried to establish some kind of order, he was warmed by the thought that for centuries his ancestors had trod the same earth as he did daily and that the people he saw around him had their roots in it too. He also looked at the parish records of baptisms and marriages, which went back to the sixteenth century. Time and again they showed that the Tocquevilles had acted as godparents to the children of the village, "a new proof of the sweet and paternal relationships that still existed in those days between the upper and lower classes, relationships that have been replaced so widely by feelings of jealousy, distrust, and often hatred."[18]

He did his best to prolong the ancient confidence between classes while modernizing its basis. When he could without being ostentatious, he eliminated local practices and traditions that set him apart from the other well-to-do inhabitants of his village. The seigneurs of Tocqueville had

[16] T. to Mrs. Grote, Oct. 1, 1856, *Corr.*, II, 342-43
[17] T. to Comtesse de Grancey, Dec. 28, 1856, *N.C.*, pp. 425-26; Loménie, *loc.cit.*, p. 422
[18] T. to Baron Hubert de Tocqueville, Feb. 23, 1857, *N.C.*, pp. 435-36

occupied the most prominent seats in the village church, and the practice had continued down to Alexis's day. During one of the periods of his residence in his château, the church was closed for general repairs. The villagers discovered when the building was reopened that the seigneurial pew had disappeared and the Tocquevilles now had a bench no better than those of the mayor and municipal council. Alexis also kept his ear open for cases of hardship. Every week at his château he had bread baked for the poor and taken to their homes so that no beggar need come to his door. One of the friends who visited him remarked that he had transformed "the former family patriciate into a truly democratic patronage."[19] Perhaps, but Tocqueville's life also recalls the ideal that Rousseau had held up to the aristocracy in his sentimental novel *La nouvelle Heloïse*: the household of the adorable Julie and her kind husband, who shunned the mundane pleasures of the city and devoted their lives to procuring the happiness of their peasants, receiving love and gratitude as their reward.

Alexis led a tranquil, happy life, his first real relaxation in years. Even a brief illness of Marie did little to spoil his contentment. "Time flies in the midst of these peaceful occupations. We find that it passes much too fast, and indeed, our life is slipping by. What a pity that one doesn't really know how to take advantage of it until one is old."[20]

His felicity was marred only by a relapse of his new-found hope for the spirit of his countrymen. In October 1856 his old feeling of "intellectual and moral isolation" seized him again. The return of discouragement with his times and his country finally drove him back to his desk. By January 1857 he was writing with something of the old ardor, but

[19] Loménie, *loc.cit.*, pp. 419-20
[20] T. to Comtesse de Grancey, Dec. 28, 1856, *N.C.*, p. 426; on Mme. de Tocqueville's illness, T. to Mme. Phillimore, Nov. 29, 1856, *ibid.*, p. 417

his energy rapidly gave way to depression. His letters, after making much of his new endeavor, ceased to speak of it after January. His thoughts turned from France to the eternal problems of human existence and the hereafter, and he suddenly felt overwhelmed by his inability to penetrate their mysteries.[21]

The project remained on his mind, however. Late in 1856 he learned that the British Museum had an extensive collection of French Revolutionary publications. He decided to use the royalties of his book to go to England. In April 1857 he went to Paris to plunge into libraries and archives, and late in June he travelled to London. At once he was pounced upon and lionized by members of society, and for a month he basked in popularity.[22] At the end of his stay a special ship of the British navy carried him directly from Portsmouth to a dock near Tocqueville. So far as research was concerned, he had accomplished little. He found that the collection of twelve hundred Revolutionary pamphlets in the British Museum was of no use because it was uncatalogued. On the other hand, thanks to special permission, he looked at the British diplomatic correspondence from Paris in the years 1788-1789, and he was able to read enough to grasp its general spirit. Later he asked for copies of two despatches, which dealt with the struggle between the Parlement of Paris and the king in 1788.[23]

[21] T. to Mme. Swetchine, Feb. 26, 1857, quoted by Redier, p. 283. Redier does not publish the entire letter; other parts can be found in A. P. F. de Falloux (ed.), *Lettres inédites de Madame Swetchine* (2nd ed., Paris, 1866), pp. 487-89. On his writing during the winter: T. to Mme. Swetchine, Oct. 20, 1856, *Corr.*, II, 350; T. to Ampère, Jan. 27, 1857, *ibid.*, pp. 363-64

[22] See the correspondence between T. and Reeve, Nov. 1856 to July 1857, *C.A.*, pp. 207-28, esp. T. to Reeve, Nov. 21, 1856 and Apr. 5, 1857, pp. 207-8, 216-18; on use of royalties, T. to Comtesse de Pizieux, Sept. 21, 1857, *N.C.*, pp. 460-61

[23] T. to Ampère, July 26, 1857, *Corr.*, II, 392; T. to Reeve, Aug. 8, 1857, *C.A.*, pp. 232-33. The documents copied are given *ibid.*, pp. 242-45

What he did acquire in England was the vision of a country in which liberty was alive:

"One finds there things entirely unknown in the rest of Europe. I was comforted by their view.

"I do not doubt that in the lower classes there exists a certain amount of hostile feeling for the other classes, but it is not evident. What one does see everywhere is the union and mutual understanding that exists among all the men who make up the enlightened classes, from the bottom of the bourgeoisie to the highest aristocracy, to defend society and direct it freely in common. I have not envied England her wealth and power, but I envy her that spirit. I breathed freely for the first time on finding myself, after so many years, outside the hatreds and class jealousies that, after being the source of all our ills, have ended by destroying our liberty."[24]

Again it cost him trouble to get back to work. During his stay in England the first telegraphic news had arrived of the Sepoy rebellion in India.[25] Marie's English blood was deeply stirred by the catastrophe, and Alexis's imagination was seized by the dangers into which the ferocity of the native troops plunged the British rulers. While a deputy in the 1840's he had made a study of the rule of the British East India Company, and this increased his interest and anxiety.[26] The Crimean War had not distracted him from his writing, but for months discussions of India and the British Empire filled his correspondence far more than did the French Revolution. As late as July 1858, when hope of completing his book was fast receding, his amazing power of prognostication was still aroused by the sight of India. "I have long thought that at the bottom of everything that

[24] T. to Corcelle, July 29, 1857, *Corr.*, II, 393-94
[25] T. to Lavergne, Sept. 4, 1857, *N.C.*, p. 459
[26] T. to Reeve, Sept. 19, 1843 and Mar. 23, 1846, *C.A.*, 72, 92-93; T. to Comtesse de Grancey, Oct. 8, 1857, *N.C.*, p. 464

is going on in that part of the Orient there is a new and general fact, a universal reaction against the European race."[27]

In the fall of 1857 he forced himself back to his task, but only because he again found the effort of work a relief from his unhappiness. The difficulty of saying something new about the Revolution continued to haunt him.[28] Gradually regular habits of work returned ("Before noon I am a writer, after noon a peasant")[29] bringing a revival of his spirits. Once more he grew hopeful for the future of France, although he continued to insist on the difficulty of establishing liberty among a people that had lost the true concept of it. He even came to admit that Napoleon III was not the worst tyrant France could find.[30]

Part of his new buoyancy was due to his success in finishing the first book of his next volume, which he announced as ready in January 1858. It was the product of two winters of work at Tocqueville and bears witness to the remarkable strength of will of the author—who could literally drive himself to compose it against an instinctive urge for rest.[31]

This book, which he did not live to publish, consists of seven chapters. In the first, Tocqueville scans the European scene in 1789 and observes the signs of moral excitement and expectancy that preceded the actual outbreak of the Revolution. Then he returns to France and deals in the following chapters with the period of what is now called the "aristocratic revolt," from 1787 to the meeting of the Estates

[27] T. to Circourt, July 19, 1858, *Corr.*, II, 448-49

[28] T. to Freslon, Nov. 5, 1857, *ibid.*, p. 416; T. to Beaumont, Nov. 20, 1857, *ibid.*, p. 417

[29] T. to Lord Hatherton, Nov. 27, 1857, *ibid.*, p. 421

[30] T. to Freslon, Jan. 12, 1858, *N.C.*, p. 478; T. to Beaumont, Feb. 27, 1858, *ibid.*, pp. 488-89; on Napoleon III, T. to Ampère, Feb. 18, 1858, *ibid.*, p. 486

[31] T. to Freslon, Jan. 12, 1858, *ibid.*, p. 478; T. to Kergorlay, Feb. 27, 1858, *Corr.*, I, 400-401

General in May 1789. In *Old Regime* he viewed 1787 as the year of the abortive royal democratic revolution. Now he sees it equally clearly as the year of the rebellion of the nobility. They acted through the Assembly of Notables and the Parlement of Paris to break the absolute power of the crown. Their revolt succeeded because the people supported them. "Hatred of arbitrary rule appeared for a moment to be the sole passion of Frenchmen, and the government the common enemy."[32]

The victory of the aristocracy became their undoing. The king in his defeat managed, albeit unintentionally, to sow seeds of discord among his people once again. This he did by calling for public expressions of opinion on the proper form in which to convoke the Estates General. As the different classes vied for preponderance in the forthcoming meeting, all the ingrained hatreds burst forth in hitherto unknown fury. The wrath of the Third Estate was deflected from the crown to the nobles (Tocqueville cites the Abbé Sieyès' famous pamphlet, *Qu'est-ce que le Tiers État?*, which called the nobles the heirs to the old Frankish invaders, foreigners to the true French nation). The imbecility of the king thus brought on the "class struggle" that was to destroy him and his whole regime.

As the meeting of the Estates General approached, a growing expectancy hushed these animosities. "Basically [the classes] do not really agree, but they try to convince themselves that they will agree. They become reconciled without making their positions clear. . . . It was only for a moment, but I doubt if ever a similar moment occurred in the life of any people. . . . A common joy filled their

[32] A.R., II, 52 (*Eur. Rev.*, p. 45). The seven chapters are given in A.R., II, 33-134 (*Eur. Rev.*, pp. 33-87)

hearts, so divided, and brought them together for a last instant before they were separated forever."[33] Even *Old Regime* did not end so tragically.

In historical insight these chapters are the equal of his earlier book, but they reveal little new about Tocqueville's concept of French history. The king's revolution had failed and was followed by the nobles' revolution, which failed also, because of class hatreds. In sum he had proved his point again, and he had not yet begun the history of the real Revolution.

Nor was he to. He had scarcely been able to work four or five months in nearly two years and had complained frequently of the difficulty of the subject. Now he had the Revolution itself before him. He wrote his lifelong friend Kergorlay in May 1858 that he was worried about the book; at the rate he was going he would never finish. His subject, he said, had to be the movement of ideas and feelings, the changes in social state, institutions, and spirit of Frenchmen. In the Revolution, Frenchmen were suffering from a strange disease, "a new and unknown virus," and he could not discover its origin.[34]

Another intimate friend recalled that in these years, "Whenever I spoke to him about the conclusion of his work he answered me more like a man who hopes to discover it than like one who already grasps it."[35] As Tocqueville himself described his condition, he was "ice bound."[36] He gives the same impression of being at a loss that he did when he was trying earlier to deal with the Revolution through the First Empire, before he went to Tours in 1853. In 1836, when he wrote the "Political and Social Condition of France," he got as far as the Revolution. At the end he

[33] *A.R.*, ii, 133, 132, 133 (*Eur. Rev.*, pp. 86, 85, 86)
[34] T. to Kergorlay, May 16, 1858, *Corr.*, i, 403-4
[35] Rémusat, *loc.cit.*, p. 805
[36] T. to Beaumont, May 21, 1858, *Corr.*, ii, 438

promised further articles on the effects of the Revolution itself.[37] They were never written. Evidently something in his constitution reacted against the subject.

Perhaps he realized intuitively that in undertaking the history of the Revolution he was facing a challenge for which his genius was not fitted. His technique was superb for dealing with a vast canvas, in which he painted social forces and class structure over a period of centuries. It was not suitable to a picture in which the role of individuals and daily occurrences was crucial. "I speak of classes, they alone should concern history," he said in *Old Regime*.[38] Book III of *Old Regime* reveals already his weakness in handling a brief period—the reign of Louis XVI—without describing individual influences. Louis, the tragic hero of the piece, is but a shadowy figure in the background. A history of the Revolution itself demanded almost peremptorily that he focus on leaders and events. Had Tocqueville continued his task, his discouragement would certainly have recurred. It has been fashionable since his death to lament the fate that kept him from finishing his history. We should instead be mercifully thankful that he was saved further sorrow and frustration. For we can learn all he really had to say from *Old Regime*, if we penetrate beneath its surface.

For some months his health, which had left him relatively carefree since the publication of his book, had again given him concern. With his condition already shaky, he went for a walk during a storm in February 1858 to watch the splendor of the winter seas breaking on the icy shores beneath

---

[37] *London and Westminster Review*, xxv (1836), 169 (also *A.R.*, i, 66). T. to J. S. Mill, Apr. 10, 1836, says he has postponed writing the second article because he has returned to writing *Democracy*: "I have at this moment *la monomanie de la 'Démocratie'*" (quoted in Friedrich Engel-Janosi, *Four Studies in French Romantic Historical Writing* [Baltimore, 1955], pp. 121, 124)

[38] *A.R.*, i, 179 (*Old Reg.*, Bk. ii, ch. xii, p. 122)

his château. The birds beating valiantly into the winds and the forces of the tempest assaulting the habitat of man recalled to him the wild raptures that had seized him in the past as he stood in this place and gazed on other storms. This time, however, the experience proved saddening, and his health took a turn for the worse after it.[39] He hoped a visit to Paris to do research would cure him, and early in the spring he made the trip. It was a failure, for he had to spend his time in bed.

He returned to Tocqueville in May. A month later he was terrified by coughing up blood, for the first time since 1850.[40] He could not recover from the shock nor from the illness. In September he visited his doctor in Paris, who immediately ordered him to return home.[41] He grew worse and once more took the trying journey to Paris. This time he was sent to Cannes, to winter beside the Mediterranean.

The voyage south turned out to be disastrous. He was already weakened by fever when he boarded the train at Paris with Mme. de Tocqueville. As the train crept along beside the Rhône River, an early blizzard struck, covering the mountains with snow, blowing icy winds down the valley, and freezing the travellers inside the primitive railroad cars. Four days elapsed before they reached the end of the line, and then the couple had to spend three more days in a carriage. When they finally reached the small house they had engaged at Cannes, Alexis was completely exhausted and Marie had fallen ill.[42]

Rest and warmth seemed briefly to restore their strength. By December Alexis had recovered enough to take walks,

[39] T. to Freslon, Mar. 5, 1858, *Corr.*, II, 436

[40] T. to Senior, June 30, 1858, *Conversations with Senior*, II, 211; T. to Mrs. Grote, July 23, 1858, *Corr.*, II, 449

[41] T. to Reeve, Sept. 25, 1858, *C.A.*, p. 275

[42] T. to Circourt, Nov. 12, 1858, *Corr.*, II, 459-60; T. to Baron Hubert de Tocqueville, Nov. 15, 1858, *N.C.*, p. 515

but January 1859 saw a relapse. Again he was spitting blood, breathing became maddeningly painful, and his mind began to wander. He snapped repeatedly at his brothers, who had come to support Marie in the crisis.[43]

In February he improved, but he was too weak to work. His sole diversions were occasional reading and the comforting correspondence of his friends. Despite the sunny and magnificent beauty of his surroundings, he was desperately homesick. To one well-wisher he replied: "I am grateful for your warm recollections of my poor Tocqueville. It has a special place in my heart; and I would far rather live under its sky, at times so gently melancholy, at others so stormy and terrible, than to breathe the most perfumed air in the world by the shores of the bluest and calmest of all seas. My thoughts are sad as they turn to it now, because I fear that its climate and my health will never become totally reconciled, and I despair of ever spending beneath my roof those long winters that seemed to me so short."[44]

For a moment in March he recovered enough to assure his friends that all would be well. But he was still too ill to see acquaintances, and the strain had completely destroyed Marie's health. Admitting to himself the full seriousness of his situation, he at last wrote his best friends, begging them to come. Beaumont and Kergorlay soon appeared. Despite their presence and the knowledge that Ampère was on his way to join their watch, his last days could not have been more painful. Marie was too ill to speak and had to use a slate to communicate with those around her. He himself was unable to talk except in a low voice. The two could be together for only brief periods.

---

[43] T. to Ampère, Dec. 30, 1858, *Corr.*, II, 465-66; T. to Edouard de Tocqueville, Feb. 17, 1859, *ibid.*, p. 473; T. to Comtesse de Tocqueville, Feb. 23, 1859, *ibid.*, p. 474

[44] T. to Bouchitte, Mar. 5, 1859, *N.C.*, p. 522

Repeatedly she urged him to confess and take communion. He was reluctant because of his lack of belief in the Christian doctrines, but at last he yielded to Marie's pleadings. The local priest administered the sacrament to both of them beside his bed early in April. Shortly thereafter, on April 16, 1859, death finally claimed him.[45] He was fifty-four years old.

He had asked to be buried in the churchyard of Tocqueville, among the people he considered his own. Overwhelmed by her loss and physically ill, Mme. de Tocqueville nevertheless determined to fulfill her self-imposed duties to the end. Supported by his close friends and relatives, she accompanied his body back across the breadth of France and saw his last wish carried out. Five years later she was laid beside him.[46]

[45] T. to Ampère, Apr. 9, 1859, *Corr.*, ii, 487-88; Beaumont "Notice," *loc.cit.*, pp. 117-18; on Tocqueville's confession and communion, Beaumont's account quoted by Chevalier in *Correspondance . . . Tocqueville . . . Gobineau*, p. 13n., and the reports of witnesses of uneven reliability collected by Redier, pp. 291-97.

[46] Ampère, *Mélanges*, p. 336; G. de Beaumont, "Avant-propos," in *N.C.*, p. iii

IX · "OLD REGIME" AS TRACT . . .

WHEN Tocqueville died, all the French public had seen of his historical writing was *Old Regime*. Shortly thereafter Gustave de Beaumont, by agreement with Mme. de Tocqueville, began to publish a comprehensive edition of his works and correspondence. The first volume, which appeared in 1861, included the two chapters on the advent of Napoleon that Tocqueville had struggled to write in 1852 before turning his attention to the old regime. Four years later a subsequent volume contained the article of 1836 on the "État social et politique de la France avant et depuis 1789," the seven chapters written after *Old Regime*, and other lesser fragments and notes accumulated on the general subject of the French Revolution. Beaumont had taken upon himself to polish the rough drafts of the seven chapters into finished literary products that he thought would do greater honor to the memory of his late friend. Only recently has M. André Jardin published a reliable version of these scattered pieces in the edition of *L'Ancien Régime et la Révolution*, put out under the patronage of the Commission nationale pour l'Édition des Œuvres d'Alexis de Tocqueville.[1]

[1] Alexis de Tocqueville, *Mélanges, fragments historiques et notes*

When Beaumont published Tocqueville's minor historical works, they caused little stir; for they seemed not to
add much to his previously expressed views on French history, and the novelty of his thoughts had already begun to
wear off. In contrast, the appearance of *Old Regime* had
turned out to be an important event in the cultural life of
France. The book revealed unknown and unexpected features of the country's past to a public that had long been
accustomed to view the interpretation of their history as
having direct bearing on contemporary developments. "It
is a new French Revolution that you unfold before our eyes,
of which we had no idea," Beaumont wrote his friend.[2] He
might better have said, "It is a new view of our own existence that you reveal." His feelings were common to many
readers.

What particularly struck them was the discovery that
France owed less to the Revolution and more to the old regime than was believed. Ampère wrote for an Italian journal: "Astonishment grips us as we come to realize through
the book of M. de Tocqueville to what an extent almost all
the things that we look upon as results or, as we like to
say, 'conquests' of the Revolution existed already in the old
regime: administrative centralization, administrative tute-
lage, administrative habits; guarantee of the civil servant
against the citizen, profusion of public offices and hunger
for them; even conscription, the supremacy of Paris, and

---

sur *l'Ancien Régime, la Révolution et l'Empire, voyages, pensées*
(*Œuvres complètes*, ed. G. de Beaumont, Vol. viii [Paris, 1865]).
On the lack of reliability of this volume, see Jardin, *loc.cit.*, p. 9. The
1861 volume has been cited in this study as "*Corr., i*" (see above, p.
10, n.1). Jardin's edition of *L'Ancien Régime* is cited above, p. 19,
n.20. The other editions of it are listed in J.-P. Mayer, "L'Influence de
l'Ancien Régime," *loc.cit.*, pp. 337-38

[2] Beaumont to T. Apr. 23, 1856, Y.T.MSS, D i b, 8e cah.

the extreme division of land. All these things existed prior to 1789."³

Readers with the most varied interests learned something that touched them closely—whether it was that greed for public office was older than the Revolution or that many peasants had been landowners under the old regime.⁴ It was an accomplishment to have disproved the belief that "the old regime and the new are above all characterized by the two opposite land tenure systems of large versus small holdings,"⁵ but the misconception died hard. In 1930 Marc Bloch still found the general view to be that the fragmentation of the French soil had not occurred until after the Revolution, when Napoleon's Civil Code established equal division of inherited estates.⁶

For most of Tocqueville's readers, the importance of these discoveries was obscured by their excitement over his account of royal centralization. "Clearly the most unexpected part of his work," according to one reviewer; "the dominant idea of his book, the thesis to which he repeatedly returns," said another. "The idea is new, and M. de Tocqueville insists on it with the relish and inevitable exaggeration that one falls into when upholding a new idea of one's own in-

³ J.-J. Ampère, review of *Old Regime* in *Revista Contemporanea* (Turin), July 25, 1856, reprinted in his *Mélanges*, II, 320-21

⁴ See the following reviews of *Old Regime*: Léon Plée, "L'Ancien Régime et la Révolution française," *Le Siècle* (Paris), July 18, 19, 21, 27, 1856 (esp. July 21); and Frédéric Passy, "L'Ancien Régime et le nouveau," *Journal des économistes*, 2ᵉ série, XIII (Jan.-Mar. 1857), 43-59 (esp. pp. 46-48) on public offices; A. Villemain, "Variétés, L'Ancien Régime et la Révolution, par M. Alexis de Tocqueville," *Journal des Débats* (Paris), July 1, 1856; Armand de Pontmartin, "Causeries littéraires," *L'Assemblée Nationale* (Paris), July 5, 12, 1856 (esp. July 12); and Eugène Despois, "L'Ancien Régime et la Révolution par M. de Tocqueville," *Revue de Paris*, XXXIX (Oct. 1856), 56-81 (esp. p. 78) on the peasants

⁵ Passy, *loc.cit.*, pp. 45-46

⁶ Marc Bloch, *Les Caractères originaux de l'histoire rurale française* (Oslo, 1931), pp. 171-72

vention."[7] Whether the readers felt that centralization was a curse or a blessing, they were willing to shift responsibility for it from the National Assembly and Napoleon to the monarchy.[8] Thus the first public reaction to *Old Regime* pointed to this as the main subject of the book: the lesson that France's centralized administration was not a product of the Revolution. This has remained the most common interpretation of the book down to the present.

It must seem strange to anyone moderately familiar with the history of France that Tocqueville's discovery came as such a surprise a century ago. The long history of the Capetian, Valois, and Bourbon dynasties has come to be centered on the story of the extension and hardening of royal authority. How was it possible that Frenchmen had to wait for *Old Regime* to discover what now seems an obvious fact? Even at the time one reviewer recognized the absurdity of the situation: "After having read this victorious demonstration, one is astonished that we have been able to overlook so evident a truth; and one wonders . . . how plain common sense did not reveal this truth to us. To say on the one hand that the French monarchy was absolute and on the other that our centralization dates from the Revolution is to state two absolutely contradictory facts."[9] The reviewer made no attempt to account for the wide misconception, and no one at the time appears to have suggested an answer. It is possible, however, to deduce the answer from the comments of the contemporary readers of *Old Regime*.

[7] Passy, *loc.cit.*, p. 51; Despois, *loc.cit.*, p. 58

[8] Pontmartin, *loc.cit.*, July 5, and Ed. Scherer, "Variétés, Alexis de Tocqueville," *Le Temps* (Paris), May 7, 1861 (a curse); B. Hauréau, "L'Ancien Régime et la Révolution," *L'Illustration, Journal Universel* (Paris), July 19, 1856 (a blessing). Other critics who laid emphasis on the theme of centralization were Villemain, *loc.cit.*, Loménie, *loc.cit.*, pp. 414-15, and Albert Gigot, "M. de Tocqueville," *Le Correspondant*, LI (1860), 690-726 (esp. p. 717).

[9] Despois, *loc.cit.*, pp. 58-59

Charles de Rémusat, a companion of Tocqueville in the former legislatures and like him now in retirement writing history, sensed that the recent upheaval in France had prepared the public for a historical revision of this kind:

"We used to believe that the question had been judged. The work of the Revolution appeared complete and its case had been won. Not ten years ago we still thought that there had been excellent reasons for replacing the entire old regime by the new condition of societies.

"But events continued their march. Many hopes were dashed, many doctrines disproved. Each party, having in turn failed, was condemned to lose confidence in itself. The promises of 1789 have again been accused of imposture. . . . Sacrifices have followed upon sacrifices, trials upon trials, and the result, precarious, incomplete, disputed, has not offered a reward commensurate with such labor. . . . What are we to think of the old regime? What are we to think of the Revolution?

"M. de Tocqueville has resolutely attacked this twofold question. . . ."[10]

To many who now shared these doubts about the Revolution, Tocqueville provided the answer they longed for. Odilon Barrot felt that his former colleague had hit the nail on the head in revealing how centralization, equality, uniformity, and the Revolution in general deprived France of "all its youth, its strength, its originality, and its liberty."[11] Edouard Laboulaye, professor of comparative government at the Collège de France, took up his pen as soon as he closed the book and wrote the author: "All that you have written about centralization has moved me, all the more since I am familiar with the monster. C'est l'infâme qu'il

---

[10] Charles de Rémusat, "L'Ancien Régime et la Révolution par M. Alexis de Tocqueville," *Revue des deux mondes*, 2ᵉ série, IV (1856), 652-70 (quotation from pp. 652-53)

[11] Barrot to T., n.d., quoted in Marcel, p. 116

faut écraser, if we wish to have liberty in our poor country."[12]

What pleased these men most was Tocqueville's proof that there were causes much older than their own day for the evils they were suffering. The liberal monk, Henri-Dominique Lacordaire, who was elected to the chair of the Academy left vacant by Tocqueville's death, said in his eulogy of his predecessor: "Tocqueville aimed to show his contemporaries that they lived unknowingly under the same regime they thought they had destroyed and that herein lay the main source of their eternal disappointments. . . . Do you know who is the inventor of this mechanism, who the creator of this servitude? It is not the Revolution, it is the old regime. It is not 1789, it is Louis XIV and Louis XV. It is not the present, it is the past."[13]

It is not we, Lacordaire meant. We liberals are not to blame for our present fix, nor are our ideals. This was the lesson of the book that the liberal opponents of the Second Empire relished. Listen to the satisfaction of another member of their group, Frédéric Passy, one of the editors of the important *Journal des économistes*:

"Liberty, for M. de Tocqueville, is the solution for all difficulties, the remedy for all ills, the source of all progress. . . . His picture of the old regime . . . is a practical example of the need for liberty. It offers at the same time a solemn atonement. On all sides liberty was accused of causing the ruin of the old regime and infecting the new. The discontents that preceded the Revolution and the excesses that sullied it were attributed to the sudden mania for being free. M. de Tocqueville has proved, on the contrary, that

[12] Laboulaye to T., July 3, 1856, quoted *ibid.*, pp. 116-17
[13] Henri-Dominique Lacordaire and F.-P.-G. Guizot, *Discours prononcés dans la séance publique tenue par l'Académie française pour la reception de M. Lacordaire, le 24 janvier 1861* (Paris, 1861), pp. 22-23

'among all the ideas and all the feelings that prepared the Revolution, the idea and taste of liberty appeared last' and 'were the first to disappear.' . . .

"Thanks to him liberty has at last been washed once and for all of any responsibility for the fall of the old regime. . . . Let us bear witness, with legitimate satisfaction, to the imposing justification that our doctrines find in history."[14]

"Continue," Laboulaye urged Tocqueville, "Continue, Sir, to make us understand and love liberty. We must hope that the country will not always be deaf and ungrateful."[15]

The reactions of these men were what cheered Tocqueville in the months after publication and convinced him that his book did "revive free and energetic feelings in discouraged souls and tired and wavering minds."[16] Believing themselves to be champions of liberty, they found in *Old Regime* the justification their wavering minds sorely needed, and they failed to observe its real conclusion: that France was destined for tyranny.

These were typical liberals of the mid-nineteenth century, who were frightened by universal suffrage and strong government. They saw in the Caesarian democracy of Napoleon III the destruction of their ideals of limited government, *laissez faire*, and legislation by responsible property owners. They had been trying ever since 1815 to obtain the kind of constitutional regime based on liberty that they desired, and repeatedly they had failed. As Rémusat said, they had begun to lose confidence in themselves.

The trouble was that they had been living in the grip of

[14] Passy, *loc.cit.*, pp. 58-59. He quotes from A.R., I, 209 (*Old Reg.*, Bk. III, ch. iii, p. 157).
[15] Laboulaye to T., July 3, 1856, quoted in Marcel, pp. 116-17. See also Villemain, *loc.cit.*; Despois, *loc.cit.*, pp. 80-81; Loménie, *loc.cit.*, pp. 418-19
[16] See above, p. 91

the Revolutionary legend—the vision of the French Revolution as a clean sweep and triumph of liberty. According to the legend, the influence of the old regime had been destroyed in 1789. By implication, the condition of France in the nineteenth century was attributable to those alive, or to their fathers, and the success of Louis Napoleon showed how utterly the partisans of liberty had failed in their appointed task. What a welcome surprise to discover that instead of being delinquent they were the victims of circumstances, of conditions inherited from the old regime! Tocqueville broke the spell that the Revolutionary legend had cast over French minds. Before he could write *Old Regime*, he had had to lay aside the legend. Now his book was freeing the French public from its hold, and the liberation came as a shock to men who had not known they were enthralled. Herein lies the reason for the minor sensation caused by the appearance of *Old Regime*.

Closely associated with the Revolutionary legend was the Napoleonic legend—the concept of the first emperor as the great lawgiver, the Solon of modern France. *Old Regime* was a blow to it too. If it was true that 1800 only re-established the old regime, which 1789 had attempted to destroy, then the achievements of 1800 were no more noteworthy than the ideals of 1789 were wrong. Perceptive Bonapartists were quick to sense the dangers to their creed present in Tocqueville's book. One who rose to defend the established belief was Adolphe de Forcade de la Roquette, a youthful member of the civil administration. Eager to impress his imperial master with his loyalty and learning, he seized the opportunity to write a lengthy review of *Old Regime* for *La Revue contemporaine*, a leading government-sponsored periodical.[17]

[17] Ad. de Forcade de la Roquette, "Le Gouvernement impérial et l'opposition nouvelle," *Revue contemporaine et athénaeum français*,

Forcade notes that despite its apparent concern with the past, *Old Regime* "does not remove us from contemporary polemics as much as one would at first suppose." He sees through to the inner meaning of the book, observing that its message is that the cause of the present situation of France lies in the nature of French society as it was formed by the old regime. He quotes the passage that ends "every time since then that we have tried to destroy absolute power, we have succeeded only in placing the head of Liberty on the body of a slave."

Forcade considers the proposition that Napoleon had merely re-established the centralization and the tyranny of the old regime as a slur against a great man. Replying heatedly, he summons Thiers to his support and quotes the latter's glowing praise of Bonaparte's reorganization of the administration. Forcade adds that Napoleon's prefects might recall the former intendants, but they were free from the financial expedients, the hocus-pocus, and the "bon plaisir" practiced by the intendants to hoodwink the royal ministers. "The great man whom the parties insist on representing as the founder of despotism took care to place the administration that he organized under the rule of law and to establish at each level of the administrative hierarchy an effective system of public surveillance and control."

In other ways *Old Regime* is unfair to the imperial accomplishments, Forcade argues. Look at the financial crisis on the eve of 1789, which Tocqueville never mentions! Forcade quotes a hairraising description of the chaos of the royal treasury that was read to the National Assembly in 1791 by one of its members. The fiscal problem was not solved by the Revolution, he maintains, it had to await the

---

xxix (1856), 5-29 (besides *Old Regime,* this reviews Charles de Rémusat, *L'Angleterre au dix-huitième siècle* [2 vols., Paris, 1856]). The quotations below are from pp. 8, 6, 13-14, 29.

coming of the Consulate. Look furthermore at the threat to liberty at the hands of equality, which so worries Tocqueville! It also worried Montesquieu (is it an accident that he cites Tocqueville's favorite philosopher?), who saw in an extreme spirit of equality the corruption of democracy. Indeed such a danger did exist, Forcade admits, but only until Napoleon's legal codes established a safe basis and a limit for equality. True liberty (again he cites Montesquieu) is found in the tranquillity of spirit that comes with freedom from the fear of one's fellow citizens. This liberty Napoleon I provided. This liberty was lacking in 1848, but was restored by Napoleon III. "Those politicians who have seen their ship run aground can now observe, without regrets or dishonor, how a more capable pilot, after saving the crew, has seized the helm and is continuing the voyage."

Can one suppose that Forcade's review was brought to the imperial attention and read with a satisfied eye? Previous to the coup of December 1851 he had been a young and little-known Parisian lawyer. In the reorganization of the Council of State that followed, he was named a maître des requêtes and promptly was sent off to be regional director of forests at Bordeaux. Born and reared in Paris, he must have received his assignment like a banishment, yet in Bordeaux he still languished in 1856 when he wrote his review of *Old Regime*. Less than a year later he was back in Paris as general director of forests. In rapid succession he became director of indirect revenues, senator, minister. It obviously did no harm, when so many publicists were in opposition to the Empire, to write intelligently in its favor.[18]

---

[18] See the articles on Forcade as well as the other reviewers of *Old Regime* in Pierre Larousse, *Grand dictionnaire universel du XIXᵉ siècle* (15 vols., Paris, 1866-76), and *La Grande encyclopédie* (31 vols., Paris, 1886-1901). The political alignment of contemporary periodicals is indicated in Eugène Hatin, *Bibliographie historique et critique de la presse périodique française* (Paris, 1866).

Nor were the emperors the only crowned heads he defended. Going back to the source of the evil as Tocqueville saw it, Forcade came to rescue the kings of France from *Old Regime*'s unfair accusations. The monarchs, when they took the measures so repugnant to the nostalgia for feudal franchises of the author of *Old Regime*, were acting in what they believed to be the best interests of France, he asserted. This was the case for Louis XIV when he assumed the control of municipal finances and for Turgot when he abolished corporations. The kings had no concerted plan to destroy liberty.

Was it pure chance that a Bonapartist should champion the work of the former kings? Forcade was not unique; Sainte-Beuve, another supporter of Napoleon III, also defended them: "In his horror of centralization the author [of *Old Regime*] is led to overlook the great advances that justice owes to Richelieu and Louis XIV. For an ordinary man or a bourgeois, was it not better to have to deal with an intendant, the representative of the king, than with the governor of a province such as the Duc d'Épernon [who dominated Guyenne during Louis XIV's minority]? Let us not condemn those to whom we owe the beginning of equality before the law and the first outline of the modern order which has freed us and our fathers and the whole third estate from this plague of minor tyrants who covered our land, from great lords down to petty gentry."[19]

Not one of the liberals commenting on *Old Regime* raised his voice to exonerate the kings. They agreed with Tocqueville that liberty suffered with the destruction of feudal and corporate privileges. They evidently felt akin in their present plight to the privileged orders under the old regime. The following comment, written by an avowed champion of the former aristocracy and enemy of the Revolution and pub-

[19] Sainte-Beuve, *Causeries de lundi*, xv, 97

lished in the moderate royalist *Assemblée Nationale*, might
well have come from their pens:

"[Tocqueville] has proved eloquently that the 'conquests
of the Revolution' were only the heritage of the old regime,
that the Revolution was not progress, that democratic equality was not liberty. He has spoken a noble language to a
tired and disillusioned generation."[20]

On the other hand, Sainte-Beuve was not alone in defending the ideal of equality. He was joined by those who out-
spokenly favored the Revolution. One of these, Léon Plée,
a director of the democratically inclined *Le Siècle*, which
was to be suppressed by imperial order in 1858, attacked
Tocqueville sharply as an enemy of the Revolution:

"He incriminates with restrained fury that passion for
equality which is the characteristic of modern times. In a
word, M. de Tocqueville is not a friend of the Revolution,
nor a panegyrist of its men, nor an approver of its acts;
he scarcely has any sympathy for the people who were
forced to make it. He has no confidence in democracy,
which he believes, unless it is accompanied by extraordinary and enduring conditions of liberty, fatally doomed to
the enervation of character."[21]

✦

Old Regime was an indictment of the Second Empire; this
fact escaped few readers in its day, and their comments on
it reflect their political alignment. But *Old Regime* was no
ordinary political tract. It forced its readers unexpectedly to
revise their view of France's past and to reassess their at-
titude toward the ideals and accomplishments of the Revo-

---

[20] Pontmartin, *loc.cit.*, July 12
[21] Plée, *loc.cit.*, July 18. Despois, *loc.cit.*, p. 67, gives a similar defense of "the people" and reveals a hatred of the aristocracy and
clergy. Despois calls himself a socialist, but he is a champion of the
Revolution of 1789.

lution. As they did so, their responses suggest that the real issue of their times was not so much the generic name of the regime under which they lived, be it monarchy, republic, or empire, but whether its touchstone was liberty or equality. This issue the French public of the 1850's found engrossing, capable of polarizing opinion and bringing together points of view not normally on speaking terms—liberal with traditionalist, Bonapartist with republican. At least this is the conclusion that appears to follow from the contemporary reactions to *Old Regime*. Men like Forcade de la Roquette, who found the Revolutionary ideals of liberty and equality equally attractive, were clearly exceptional.

X ... AND AS HISTORY

TOCQUEVILLE'S contemporaries never looked upon *Old Regime* as merely a tract for the times. It was good history, destroying misconceptions of their past. As a work of history it has remained popular ever since.

Later historians have modified the picture it presents. Tocqueville's belief that the aristocracy had never been weaker or more easy to gain entrance to than just before the Revolution has been upset by the discovery of the "feudal reaction" in the eighteenth century: the increasing grip of lords over peasants and the hardening of class lines.[1] The nobles at the same time regained control of the royal administration; intendants ceased to be "of humble extraction."[2] Tocqueville made the error of believing that the aristocracy of 1789 was still as Louis XIV left it.

Other errors, which arose partly from Tocqueville's lack of interest in economic questions noted by the Bonapartist Forcade, have also come to light. *Old Regime* assumes that the hardships of peasant land tenure resulted almost

[1] See Bloch, pp. 131-54, 217-37; Georges Lefebvre, *The Coming of the French Revolution*, trans. R. R. Palmer (Princeton, 1947), pp. 7-20, 131-42; Elinor Barber, *The Bourgeoisie in 18th Century France* (Princeton, 1955), pp. 98-140; Robert Forster, *The Nobility of Toulouse in the Eighteenth Century* (Baltimore, 1960), pp. 47-66

[2] Paul Ardascheff, *Les Intendants de province sous Louis XVI* (Paris, 1909), pp. 1-82, esp. pp. 25-26, where he corrects Tocqueville

exclusively from the remnants of the feudal and manorial system. It overlooks the large number of tenant farmers, sharecroppers, and agricultural laborers, whose plight Lefebvre has shown to have arisen from modern contractual relations with the landowners and who benefited little from the abolition of feudalism by the Revolution.[3] The role of royal financial difficulties in bringing about the collapse of the monarchy has been assigned much greater importance than Tocqueville gave it. C.-E. Labrousse has clarified the fiscal problem by describing how the price decline that lasted from 1778 to 1787 dried up the sources of royal income when they were most needed to meet the debts incurred in the War of American Independence.[4]

Finally, the anathema cast by Burke on the philosophes and echoed uncritically by Tocqueville—the accusation that they popularized abstract speculation on political problems

[3] Georges Lefebvre, *Questions agraires au temps de la terreur* (Paris, 1954), esp. pp. 91-114, and "La Révolution française et les paysans," in his *Études sur la Révolution française* (Paris, 1954), pp. 246-68

[4] C.-E. Labrousse, *La Crise de l'économie française à la fin de l'Ancien Régime et au début de la Révolution,* Vol. i (Paris, 1944), "Introduction générale," pp. xxxii-xlviii, esp. pp. xlii-xlv. See also C.-E. Labrousse, *Esquisse du mouvement des prix et des revenus en France au XVIIIe siècle* (2 vols., Paris, 1933). The criticisms levelled at Labrousse's interpretation of the economic cycles of the eighteenth century by David E. Landes and André Danière do not include this part of Labrousse's conclusions (Landes "The Statistical Study of French Crises," *Journal of Economic History,* X [1950], 195-211; Danière, "Feudal Incomes and Demand Elasticity for Bread in Late Eighteenth-Century France," *ibid.,* XVIII [1958], 317-31; Landes, "Reply to Mr. Danière and Some Reflections on the Debate," *ibid.,* pp. 331-38). On the effect of the American war on royal finances see also Louis Gottschalk, *The Place of the American Revolution in the Causal Pattern of the French Revolution* (Easton, Pa., 1948), esp. pp. 9-11 (reprinted in Herman Ausubel [ed.], *The Making of Modern Europe,* Vol. 1 [New York, 1951], pp. 494-510). Tocqueville was aware that the royal debt helped turn public opinion against the regime of Louis XVI (*A.R.,* i, 225 [*Old Reg.,* Bk. iii, ch. iv, pp. 178-79]), and that the bad harvest of 1788 was an immediate cause of the Revolution (*A.R.,* ii, 127 [*Eur. Rev.,* p. 83]).

because they lacked personal contact with government and administration—has largely been washed away by more attentive and less prejudiced investigators like Daniel Mornet and Peter Gay.[5]

These corrections do not discredit *Old Regime*. The limits of human labor prevent an historical work of such wide scope from resting on a complete investigation of the available sources. Historical research represents a constant process of accumulation and revision of information about the past, and Tocqueville added more than most historians to the resulting store of knowledge.

Where *Old Regime* can justly be found wanting is in those conclusions that reversed its author's previous sounder judgment. These, as has been seen, were its hostile verdict on the role of the kings and its failure to take into account the influence of foreign wars on the growth of the absolute state. Almost at once the Bonapartists jumped on the first of these weaknesses. The second took longer to set aright.

According to Eduard Fueter, most French and English historians in the generation before 1870 failed to give due weight to the influence of external forces on the evolution of their countries.[6] The disaster of the Franco-Prussian War awakened French historians to the importance of diplomatic and military history. Out of this new interest came the monumental work of Albert Sorel, *L'Europe et la Révolution française*, published between 1885 and 1904.

[5] Daniel Mornet, *La Pensée française au XVIIIe siècle* (Paris, 1926), pp. 113-19, is directed against Tocqueville and Taine. See also his *Les Origines intellectuelles de la Révolution française* (Paris, 1933), pp. 112-19 and 243-51, which shows both the speculative and practical sides of the philosophes, and his *Rousseau, l'homme et l'oeuvre* (Paris, 1950), pp. 111-12, which points out the influence of the example of Geneva on the ideas of the *Contrat social*. Peter Gay, *Voltaire's Politics, the Poet as Realist* (Princeton, 1959), pp. 7-18, specifically refutes Tocqueville.
[6] Eduard Fueter, *Geschichte der neueren Historiographie* (Munich, 1911), p. 557

Sorel's basic argument is remarkably parallel to that of *Old Regime*. Like Tocqueville, he believed that the legacy of the monarchy frustrated the high aims of the Revolution. He did not, however, blame the domestic but the foreign policy of the kings. Eight centuries of royal activity had ingrained in French minds the urge for expansion, both territorially and ideologically, Sorel argued; and this urge, taken over unconsciously and applied by the Revolutionaries, involved them in foreign wars that eventually undid the Revolution.

His explanation for the overthrow of the Revolution nevertheless led him to reassert the influence of outside danger on the constitutional evolution of France. The French failure to achieve parliamentary liberty ceased to be the fault of the kings and became the effect of France's geographical position, open to attack from hostile neighbors:

"It was in the periods of disorder and anarchy that the English people asserted their major claims against their crown. The French people in similar cases had neither the freedom nor the leisure so to act. They might have taken advantage of their dissensions to shackle their king, but the foreigner would already have seized the opportunity to shackle the French themselves. They put first things first, and the spirit of national independence prevailed over the desire for public liberty."[7]

The masters of French history have accepted these revisions in Tocqueville's interpretation, but they have not thereby lost sight of his valuable discoveries. Take, for example, Roland Mousnier, who stands at the head of the students of sixteenth- and seventeenth-century France. He has observed that the overriding factors affecting the old regime were the constant threats of foreign invasion and

[7] Albert Sorel, *L'Europe et la Révolution française*, Vol. I (3d ed., Paris, 1893), p. 191

domestic discord. The only hope for French freedom was the authority of the king, for only he could protect his ordinary subjects from foreign enemies and plundering aristocrats. "One must realize this truth, in such a state of society, the true guarantee of rights was the sovereignty of the king."[8] While thus implicitly rejecting Tocqueville's antimonarchic bias, Mousnier nevertheless speaks as a commonplace of "the centralizing and to a certain extent egalitarian revolution of the absolute monarchy."[9]

Lefebvre is another case in point. In his introduction to *Old Regime* he directs his strongest criticism at Tocqueville's failure to appreciate the influence of foreign dangers upon the centralization of France, not only during the former monarchy but in the Revolution itself. Lefebvre points out that Tocqueville's unpublished notes reveal almost complete lack of interest in the Terror. Tocqueville never saw that centralization was revived well before Napoleon by the Committee of Public Safety in 1793 in the face of foreign invasion. "One must recognize that it is a surprising gap for a sociologist and a historian not to have taken war sufficiently into account in the lives of the French." Lefebvre nevertheless sees in Tocqueville "an eminent representative of our discipline." "Let him be praised for having implicitly proclaimed that without erudition there is no history, and that in order to master the facts, we must first determine them in the most precise manner possible."[10] One senses that Lefebvre looks upon Tocqueville

[8] Roland Mousnier, "Comment les Français du XVIIe siècle voyaient la constitution," *Le XVIIe siècle: bulletin de la Société d'Étude du XVIIe Siècle*, IV (1955), 28. See also his "Quelques raisons de la Fronde, les causes des journées révolutionnaires parisiennes de 1648," *ibid.*, I (1949), pp. 33-78, esp. pp. 55-58.

[9] Mousnier, "Quelques raisons de la Fronde," *loc.cit.*, p. 55

[10] Quotations from Lefebvre, "Introduction," *loc.cit.*, p. 30, and G. Lefebvre, "À propos de Tocqueville," *Annales historiques de la Révolution française*, XXVII (1955), 314-15 and 321. In many ways the latter is a better study of Tocqueville's history than Lefebvre's introduction to *Old Regime*.

as a kindred spirit, a forerunner in finding the explanation of France's past in the evolution of its social classes. "Positive" history he calls *Old Regime*.[11] "Scientific," says another contemporary French scholar.[12] Can Frenchmen offer higher praise?

The "positive" or "scientific" nature of Tocqueville's writing cannot alone account for the continuing popularity of *Old Regime* with a wide public. Most historical works based on lengthy investigation eventually see their conclusions incorporated into later and more "up-to-date" histories, while the works themselves repose quietly on the shelves of library stacks, undisturbed save by the occasional dustcloth of an attendant or the curious fingers of a specialist. If *Old Regime* is read today in popular editions, it is not primarily because of the lengthy research that went into it.

One reason is simply that it is a pleasure to read. Its brevity and the dignified simplicity of its language, both so different from the style of most nineteenth-century historians, have strong appeal for our less leisurely age.

But the main cause of the popularity of *Old Regime*, one suspects, is that its discoveries do not apply only to the old regime in France. Readers sense that they have enduring significance for all persons whom the Revolution has since affected. Because of its lack of clarity, few who lay aside *Old Regime* after a first reading could say exactly what this significance is—different readers will think of different passages—yet they know that its author is no ordinary historian.

One can guess that in most cases they are being moved by *Old Regime*'s deepest level of meaning, what this study

[11] Lefebvre, "Introduction," *loc.cit.*, p. 19 speaks of his "sérénité positive," p. 23 of his "méthode positive."

[12] Georges Gojat, "Les Corps intermédiaires et la décentralisation dans l'oeuvre de Tocqueville," in Robert Pelloux (ed.), *Libéralisme, traditionalisme, décentralisation* ("Cahiers de la Fondation nationale des Sciences politiques," No. 31) (Paris, 1952), pp. 3, 15

has called the ocean current. More than attention to detail gives this current its force. There is, at least in America, a growing recognition of another quality inherent in historical genius: sensitivity to human relations and problems, beginning with those that the historian experiences first-hand. We have come to feel that the greater the ability of an historian to understand his own society, the more convincingly is he able to reconstruct the past. This side of historical genius verges on the inspiration of the poet.[13] Tocqueville had an extraordinary capacity to appreciate the problems of his day, in America and in France, and this capacity enabled him to perceive the lessons of history beyond the ability of most men, however deeply they delve into archives.

First of all he saw that the Revolution was not simply a French phenomenon. As he says in the foreword to *Old Regime*, his aim was to find out why the Revolution, which threatened everywhere, exploded first in France and had in France different characteristics from elsewhere. Everywhere in the West the same revolution was in progress, and that revolution consisted of the achievement of democracy.

The aim of the Revolution, he saw furthermore, was not anarchy or irreligion, as conservatives lamented who were longing for the imagined stability of the old order. It was not simply liberty either, as the liberal defenders of the Revolution insisted, fearful of the ravages of equality and socialism; nor was it equality alone, as mid-nineteenth-cen-

[13] See Louis Gottschalk, "The Historian's Use of Generalization," in Leonard D. White (ed.), *The State of the Social Sciences* (Chicago, 1956), pp. 442-43. In an appreciation of Tocqueville as an historian, Marcel Reinhard expresses much the same idea when he praises Tocqueville for having the rare "gifts of an essayist" as well as being a careful investigator ("Tocqueville historien de la Révolution," *Annales historiques de la Révolution française*, XXXII [1960], 257-65, esp. p. 265).

tury democrats asserted, decrying the social evils of unchecked economic liberty. Concerned with democracy as
an ideal toward which men were everywhere striving, and
not as a political system embodied in any actual contemporary society, even America, Tocqueville conceived that
the ideal could be approached only if men, while destroying
privilege and achieving political equality (and also a measure of economic equality, which he felt was inevitable in
democracy), preserved individual liberty and thus protected the citizen against an all-powerful state. Without the
guarantee of liberty, he realized that democracy could lead
to various forms of despotism. *Democracy in America* describes the danger of the tyranny of a majority acting
through an uncontrolled political assembly. *Old Regime* is
a response to the Caesarian democracy of the Second Empire. Events since Tocqueville's day have taught us that
an unscrupulous minority can use either type of democratic
tyranny to subvert a free people.

Many democrats have smiled at Tocqueville's wistful
recollection of the blessings of aristocracy defending its inferiors against royal tyranny, and have suggested that his
own noble blood clouded his normally clear vision. It is
true that historically the French nobles offered little support
to freedom under the old regime, but Tocqueville was well
aware of this fact. He denied that the French nobility was
an "aristocracy," saying that it had degenerated into a
"caste." No more than in the case of democracy was his concept of aristocracy associated with any historical example
(although the English upper class came close to his ideal).
For Tocqueville, aristocracy meant a society based on social
and political inequality such as had developed in western
Europe after the collapse of the Roman Empire.

Considered in these terms, his desire to preserve the essential qualities of aristocracy is more than wishful anti-

quarianism. Separate legal status and delegated political authority gave the great lords of the middle ages the ability to prevent excessive extension of royal power. Whatever attributions the kings might like to claim in theory, in practice they had to recognize the ability of their vassals to resist their encroachments. As time went on, not only nobles but cities, guilds, even royal officials, had privileges granted to them by the kings, who, ever needful of money, often received monetary payments in return. Privileges were looked upon as a kind of property, and their guarantee was a forerunner of the right of property upheld by the French Revolutionaries and later liberals. According to tradition the king could not unilaterally violate these agreements. He was not despotic, and despite all the extension of royal authority, with its leveling tendency, the existence of "aristocratic" privileges never permitted the king to become a despot under the old regime. There was, as Tocqueville pointed out, "a strange kind of liberty" which let every group— except the rural people—hold up its head before the royal officials. It was this kind of liberty which the parlements of France aimed to protect when, from the sixteenth century on, they insisted that the king respect the "fundamental laws" of the monarchy, thereby preventing him, for instance, from equalizing the tax burden among provinces and social classes. By the eighteenth century the parlements were the main champions of the *thèse nobiliaire*, the aristocratic view of government which insisted that the king rule through established bodies and respect their rights.

The democratic revolution involved the destruction of the privileges of aristocratic society in the name of equality, but the objective of those who conceived it was not to put an end to the checks on the powers of government. If all the citizens were to be equal before the law (and the tax collector), the government too was to be bound by law. Can one not say that, in a sense, the equality of the democratic ideal meant not the abolition of privileges but the extension of their basic element—the guarantee of certain rights against infringement by the government—to all citizens in equal measure? Privileges of corporate bodies before the king were to be converted into rights of the individual vis-à-vis the body of the citizens. The resulting democratic liberty was to be spelled out in declarations of the rights of man and incorporated in written constitutions, the "fundamental laws" of the new societies.

Tocqueville never described the development in precisely these terms. Coming close to them in 1836 he wrote: "According to the modern notion of liberty, the democratic notion, I make bold to say the just notion of liberty, each man, being presumed to have received from nature the necessary lights to guide his actions, brings with him into this world an equal and imprescriptible right to live independent of his equals in everything that concerns only himself and to determine his own destiny as he sees fit."[14]

"Rights must be given to every citizen, or none at all to anyone," he said in *Democracy*. The ideal of 1789, according to *Old Regime*, had been to give rights to everyone; in that year "love of equality and love of liberty shared [French] hearts." Liberty was the essence of aristocratic society and equality that of democratic society, but, Tocqueville argued, unless democracy could take over the liberty of aristocracy and join it to political equality, it could not fulfil the aims of the Revolutionaries of '89, who "wished to found not only democratic institutions but free institutions."[15]

The great challenge of the West in modern times has been to establish such institutions, to maintain freedom

[14] A.R., I, 62
[15] See above, pp. 38 & 85

(that is, government bound by laws) while achieving political equality. To Tocqueville it seemed that France had been unable to do so. A decade after the ideal of 1789 was proclaimed, it was dead. And every attempt thereafter to give it new life had failed, until the fall of the Second Republic convinced him that France could never long be both democratic and free. He wrote *Old Regime* to explain France's failure.

He found the answer in "the feelings, the beliefs, the ideas, the habits of heart and mind" of Frenchmen, whose origin he traced to the old regime. Tocqueville's phrase describes what has frequently been called "national character." The problem of national character has especial appeal for Americans, who have always been eager to explain the differences we feel between ourselves and other peoples by our own character and its influence on our political evolution. One thinks of the recent psychological and economic explanations of the American character provided by David Riesman and David Potter; one recalls the time-honored theories of George Bancroft, who attributed to divine providence the superior qualities he found in his countrymen, and Frederick Jackson Turner, who assigned to the presence of the frontier the predominant role in forming our democracy.[16] Having himself analyzed the characteristics of Americans in his first book, Tocqueville was now trying to do the same for Frenchmen, for he believed that the difference

[16] David Riesman and others, *The Lonely Crowd, a Study of the Changing American Character* (New Haven, 1950); David M. Potter, *People of Plenty, Economic Abundance and the American Character* (Chicago, 1954); George Bancroft, *History of the United States from the Discovery of the American Continent* (10 vols., Boston, 1834-75); Frederick Jackson Turner, "The Significance of the Frontier in American History," read before the American Historical Association in 1893 and published, among other places, in his *The Frontier in American History* (New York, 1920). Potter gives a rapid and penetrating survey of the treatment of national character by American and other historians, pp. 3-31.

in character was the answer to that knotty problem that has also long engrossed English and American Francophiles: Why did France not follow the political evolution of the Anglo-Saxon countries? The character of Americans, he felt, caused them to pull in the reins of their individual ambitions before overstepping the bounds beyond which they would trespass on the rights of others and harm the welfare of the republic. More down-to-earth than Bancroft, more subtle than Turner, he saw the origin of this spirit of self-restraint in our religious feelings, habit of association, and reverence for the law, and more indirectly in our institutions and geographic setting. He found much the same spirit in England—although here he believed an enlightened aristocracy was the agent for transmitting medieval liberty to modern times. This spirit, Tocqueville bitterly concluded in his second great work, had been crushed out of the French people by the vicious fiscal policies of the former kings, which turned group against group and class against class.

"[Frenchmen of his day, he found], being no longer attached to each other by any tie of caste, class, association, or family, are only too inclined to concern themselves entirely with their particular interests, too given to thinking always of themselves alone and to retreating into a narrow individualism where all public virtue is stifled."[17] Unchecked individualism in Frenchmen killed the "virtue" that Montesquieu, Rousseau, and Tocqueville agreed was necessary to keep democracy from deteriorating into despotism.

The analysis of the French character and its origins is what most distinguishes *Old Regime* from the rest of Tocqueville's writing. *Old Regime* expresses the same political philosophy as his previous works: we have seen that *Democracy* provides the key to the philosophy of *Old Regime*. Both books seek to explain the success or failure of de-

[17] A.R., I, 74 (*Old Reg.*, Foreword, p. xiii)

mocracy by studying national character; but the first is primarily the product of direct personal observation of the United States, whereas the second seeks the explanation of French character in the past as far back as the middle ages. *Old Regime* is truly historical, based on extensive research in archives and motivated by the belief that the present is understood through the past. At the same time it deals with the most elemental problems of French life as they were revealed to Tocqueville by his political philosophy and his comprehension of the world around him. The combination of these qualities makes *Old Regime* a brilliant work of history.

From the vantage point of the second half of the twentieth century, we can give Tocqueville's estimate of his country's character and prospects a test not available to him: trial by later events. In his own day Frenchmen were indeed divided between those who championed liberty and feared equality and those who worshipped equality and distrusted liberty; that would appear to be the lesson of the contemporary reaction to *Old Regime*. In his unfriendly review, the Bonapartist Forcade de la Roquette maintained that the Second Empire had reconciled the two, but few in the 1850's would have agreed with him. (Tocqueville, when playing the role of political leader instead of historian, saw himself as a protagonist of liberty. The coming of equality he accepted without enthusiasm as the will of God, who was beyond needing human partisans.)

So long as the various supporters of liberty and equality could not see that their objectives were complementary, instead of irreconcilable, France's house would continue divided. A person who understood the challenge and undertook to meet it was Émile Ollivier. Shortly before Tocqueville's death he was elected to the Legislative Body as a republican opponent of the empire. He defined his program as: "Liberty but also democracy. Without liberty, democracy is nothing but despotism. Without democracy, liberty is nothing but privilege."[18] Ollivier was willing to come to terms with Bonapartist rule, provided Caesar would make room for Cicero and Cato. Incessantly he strove to augment the power of the legislature. In the end he was largely responsible for forging the "liberal empire" of the late 1860's, which united the equality of universal suffrage with the liberty of parliamentary government. Both features were taken over by the Third Republic, and France appeared at last to have reached the goal of free democracy. Events had belied Tocqueville's gloomy judgment.

France's reaction to the nightmare of the Paris Commune showed where he had erred. In 1871, as in 1848, bourgeois liberals found a shield in the votes of the peasants against the threat they saw to property and other rights of the individual in the rising of the Parisian populace. The establishment and the continued stability of the Third Republic were made possible largely by the support of the peasants —the descendants of the common people of the countryside who alone in the old regime, according to Tocqueville, had lost all ability to hold their heads erect before royal officials. Yet, as Tocqueville discovered, many of the small landholdings that made the peasants champions of individual rights in the nineteenth century had their origin before the Revolution. Marc Bloch has shown that, once the ravages of the Black Death and the Hundred Years War permitted the peasants to acquire their holdings, France continued to be a country of small farms because the solicitous agents of the kings protected the peasantry from the encroachments of land-hungry nobles and bourgeois.[19]

[18] Émile Ollivier's unpublished diary, 1861, quoted in English by Theodore Zeldin, *The Political System of Napoleon III* (London, 1958), p. 125
[19] Bloch, p. 139. See also pp. 192-94

The perils of centralization worried Tocqueville too exclusively for him to recognize the kings' great service to the future of liberty and private property in France when, out of interest in the welfare of the largest class of taxpayers, they used their authority to shelter the peasant landholders.

But how far wrong was he really? If the peasants saved France from the Paris radicals in 1848 and 1871, they showed in 1851 that they were quite susceptible to the blandishments of Louis Napoleon. Tocqueville wrote *Old Regime* to explain the Second Empire, a phenomenon in which he now found a more permanent threat to French liberty than the popular democracy of the February Revolution. After Louis Napoleon's coup he wrote Beaumont: ". . . Not that I am convinced that this country is destined never again to see constitutional institutions; but will it see them last, them or any others? We are made of sand. One should not ask whether we shall remain stationary but only what are the winds that will blow us about."[20]

The Third Republic, after its hopeful beginning, eventually came to an end in narrow party rivalries and profound spiritual disunion. Two decades later the leaders and citizens of the Fourth Republic proved unable to unite behind any rational policy that would solve the urgent needs of their country. The resulting paralysis led France finally in both cases to "fall under the unlimited authority of a single man." All these still vivid events suggest that Tocqueville's analysis of the French character as containing irreconcilable internal dissensions that prevent voluntary cooperation for the common good was truly profound. It accounts not only for the end of the old regime and for the occurrences of his own day but for those of a century after his death. Tocqueville's explanation of the difference between the evolution of democracy among the French and

[20] See above, p. 17

English speaking peoples is not the only possible one—there are other reasons than differences of national character, such as the nearness of hostile neighbors—but it is one of the most brilliant and convincing ever conceived.

His explanation does even more. It exemplifies the culminating point of his understanding of the democratic revolution. This is that liberty and equality, which must coexist in a just democracy, cannot live together without community spirit, without "the habit of [citizens] acting together regularly and watching out for their own defense"; without what Montesquieu and Rousseau called "virtue" and the French Revolution called "Fraternity."

As we look about, not only at France and the West as Tocqueville was bound to do in his day, but at the whole world, the need for democratic government to be based on the union of "Liberty, Equality, and Fraternity" seems as true as it did one hundred or two hundred years ago. We are apt to forget how cogent was the best of the philosophy of the men of the eighteenth century who participated in the early stages of the democratic revolution. Tocqueville had the genius to appreciate the profound political insights of the Enlightenment and restate them in a way that can still move men who a century and more after him carry on the same struggle.

FIRST REFERENCES

The complete title and publication information of works cited in more than one chapter can be found in the first references to these works as indicated below.

Ampère, *Correspondance*, 26, n.42
Ampère, *Mélanges*, 14, n.7
Beaumont, "Notice," 14, n.7
Bloch, 109, n.6
Gargan, *Alexis de Tocqueville*, 13, n.6
Jardin, 30, n.1
Lefebvre, "Introduction," 30, n.1
Loménie, 21, n.25
Marcel, 90, n.4
Mayer, 30, n.1
Palmer, *Age of the Democratic Revolution*, 39, n.15
Pierson, 15, n.9
Redier, 15, n.9
Rémusat, "De l'esprit de réaction," 39, n.16
Sainte-Beuve, *Causeries de lundi*, 67, n.5

Sainte-Beuve, *Nouveaux lundis*, 11, n.2
Tocqueville
  A.R., 19, n.20
  C.A., 14, n.7
  Conversations with Senior, 13, n.6
  Corr., 10, n.1
  Correspondance . . . Tocqueville . . . Gobineau, 26, n.41
  De la démocratie, 12, n.3
  Democracy, 12, n.3
  Eur. Rev., 49, n.10
  N.C., 7, n.2
  Old Reg., 31, n.2
  "Political and Social Condition of France," 23, n.35
  "Reflections on English History," 40, n.18
  Y.T.MSS, 10, n.1

INDEX

47; in old regime, 38, 50, 52, 57, 64, 82-83; Louis XVI re-establishes, 60-61
Loménie, Louis de, 85n
Louis XIV, 117
Louis XV, 65
Louis XVI, 65, 85, 88, 98, 103; attempts to reform, 59-61; in 1787-89, 101-02
Louis Napoleon, *see* Napoleon III
Louis Philippe, 40, 69

Malesherbes, Lamoignon de, 65, 88
Mason, Jeremiah, 42
Mathiez, Albert, 9
Mayer, J.-P., 10, 30n
Mellon, Stanley, 68
monarchy, 38-39
Montesquieu, 36, 116; on democracy, 48-49, 131; T.'s view of, 48, 54, 65
Mornet, Daniel, 122
Mottley, Mary, *see* Tocqueville, Mme. de
Mousnier, Roland, 123-24

Napoleon I, 15-16; T.'s view of, 19, 63, 67-68, 71-73; legend, 69-72, 76, 114. *See also* First Empire; Tocqueville, Alexis de, *Napoleon I, chapters on*
Napoleon III, 31, 100, 113-14, 116; as Louis Napoleon Bonaparte, 13, 19, 68-69, 74, 134. *See also coup d'état* (1851), Second Empire
national character, 130-35. *See also* feelings, beliefs, ideas
natural law, 57-58
nobility, *see* aristocracy

Old Regime, *see* Tocqueville, Alexis de, *L'Ancien Régime et la Révolution*
Ollivier, Émile, 132-33

Palmer, R. R., 38, 65
Paris, T.'s visits to, 22, 27, 28,

74-75, 98, 104; growth in old regime, 51
Parlement of Paris, 98, 101
parlements, 57, 59, 65, 85. *See also* courts
Passy, Frédéric, 112
patriotism, 48
Pays d'états, *see* estates, provincial
peasants, 50, 52, 55, 60, 120-21, 133-34
philosophy of 18th century, 32, 43-44, 56-58
physiocrats, 32, 57-58
plebiscites, 16-17
Plée, Léon, 118
"Political and Social Condition of France," *see* Tocqueville, Alexis de
Potter, David, 130
prefects, 33, 70
provincial assemblies, 60
provincial government, *see* local self-government in old regime

Reeve, Henry, 29
religion, in France, 43, 58-59, 86; in U.S., 47, 59. *See also* Tocqueville, Alexis de, religious beliefs
Rémusat, Charles de, 111, 113
Revolution of 1848, 12-13
Riesman, David, 130
Rousseau, 48-49, 97, 131
Royer-Collard, Pierre-Paul, 39

Saint-Cyr, 5-8, 23-26
Sainte-Beuve, Charles-Augustin, 10-11, 67, 77, 86-87, 117
sale of offices, 52, 54, 128
Second Empire, 8, 22, 31, 93-94. *See also* Napoleon III
Second Republic, 11-12, 36. *See also coup d'état* (1851), Napoleon III
seigneurs, 50, 65
Sieyès, Abbé, 101
Sorel, Albert, 122-23
Sorrento, 15, 18-20, 74

taille, 52, 79-80
Taine, Hippolyte, 9, 58, 62